The Personality of Chaucer

The Personality of Chaucer

Edward Wagenknecht

University of Oklahoma Press
Norman

RECENT BOOKS BY EDWARD WAGENKNECHT

Nathaniel Hawthorne, Man and Writer (New York, 1961)
Mark Twain: The Man and His Work (Norman, 1961, 1967)
Washington Irving: Moderation Displayed (New York, 1962)
The Movies in the Age of Innocence (Norman, 1962)
Edgar Allan Poe: The Man Behind the Legend (New York, 1963)
Chicago (Norman, 1964)
Seven Daughters of the Theater (Norman, 1964)
Harriet Beecher Stowe: The Known and the Unknown (New York, 1965)
Dickens and the Scandalmongers: Essays in Criticism (Norman, 1965)
The Man Charles Dickens: A Victorian Portrait (Norman, 1966)
Henry Wadsworth Longfellow: Portrait of an American Humanist
(New York, 1966)
Merely Players (Norman, 1966)
John Greenleaf Whittier: A Portrait in Paradox (New York, 1967)
The Personality of Chaucer (Norman, 1968)

LIBRARY OF CONGRESS CATALOG CARD NUMBER: 67–24621

For my son Robert and Therese, his wife

PREFACE

Nobody ever taught me anything about the modern literature with which my writing has been mainly concerned. What ever I know about it I learned on my own. But when it comes to Chaucer and Shakespeare I was taught by the best, and if I have ever done any decent teaching of my own it has been in courses devoted to these masters. Perhaps that is the reason why I have not been permitted to teach either of them for many years.

The most stimulating course I ever took in my life was Edith Rickert's advanced Chaucer course, "English 237B," at the University of Chicago during the Autumn Quarter, 1923. Edith Rickert was much the greatest teacher I ever had, and I think she was the only person I have ever known who was both a great teacher and a great scholar, and in whom these two faculties reinforced and enriched each other, instead of pulling in opposite directions as they so often do. She was also a woman of much beauty and charm and of extraordinary patience and kindness, and she established the kind of personal relationship with her students that Chaucer's Clerk would have understood. She never relaxed her standards for you, no matter how well she knew you, but though you realized that you would have died if all your teachers had worked you as hard as she did, you submitted gladly to her, partly because you wished to please her but more because she had given you such a vision of what scholarship can be that, for the time being at least, she caused you to match her own devotion to it. And if that is not great teaching, then I do not know what is.

There were only three persons in the class. I was one. The second was Clark H. Slover, who was destined to run through a brief, brilliant, and somewhat erratic academic career. And the third was a pleasant, middle-aged lady who to the last day of the course addressed the instructor as "Dr. Ricketts" and remained firmly of the opinion that "The Parlement of Foules" meant the parliament of fools. And to the last day of the course, her questions—which were many—were answered with the same exquisite courtesy as Slover's or mine.

I was just then developing my interest in psychography, and when the time came to choose a subject for a term paper, it was inevitable that I should wish to try my hand at Chaucer's personality, though I was well aware of the difficulties involved in attempting to apply the psychographic method to a writer so remote in time, who had left us none of the materials—letters, journals, etc.—upon which the psychographer relies in dealing with more modern figures. But Miss Rickert was always adventurous in matters of scholarship, and though she distressed me by taking a rather dim view of "myn owene maister deere," Gamaliel Bradford, she was eager to have me try the experiment. "It is not research," she said, "but it is quite as important."

When I had finished my paper, she liked it well enough to turn it over to her great friend, the chairman of the department, John Matthews Manly, with whom she was to edit the great edition of *The Canterbury Tales* over which I am sure she worked herself to death. Manly, who had himself tried something like my Chaucer enterprise with Shakespeare,[1] was just on the eve of his

---

[1] "Shakespeare Himself," in *A Memorial Volume to Shakespeare and Harvey.* Ed. by A. C. Judson, J. T. Patterson, and J. F. Royster. *University of Texas Bulletin,* No. 1701 (January 1, 1917).

departure for Boston to give the Lowell Lectures which became *Some New Light on Chaucer* (Holt, 1926), and when he left he took my paper with him. This was the greatest compliment I had yet received, and I am not sure that it has been surpassed since.

Of course we all recognized the purely tentative character of my essay, nobody more than I, who ended the Foreword with the sentence: "Perhaps some day the colors may be heightened and the blank spaces filled in." These words were written many years ago, but at last the time has come.

Not, of course, that I am under the illusion that I have now painted a full-length portrait of Chaucer. Nobody will ever be able to do that: the material is simply not available. Much of my original outline has survived, but I have, I think, digested a great deal of scholarship which did not exist when I first became interested in the subject, and I hope, too, that my study is now somewhat more mature in its outlook and more finished in its technique. Nevertheless there is still much that I have been obliged to leave to inference, and I have said "I believe" or "it would appear" or "it seems to me" much more often than I should be willing to do it in a book dealing with a nineteenth- or twentieth-century writer.

The heroic pioneer attempt at a Chaucer bibliography was Eleanor P. Hammond's *Chaucer: A Bibliographical Manual* (Macmillan, 1908). D. D. Griffith supplemented this with his *Bibliography of Chaucer, 1908–1953*, published by the University of Washington Press in 1955. The same publisher has now announced a supplement to Griffith by William R. Crawford for publication in the spring of 1967, but this has not been available in time for me to make use of it.

It is to Hammond and Griffith and to the seasonal bibliographies in *PMLA* and elsewhere that I must refer the reader who would ask after my credentials; I cannot reproduce them here. I might of course have included a brief list of important modern studies of Chaucer, but since every one who is likely to read my book will be as familiar with these works as I am, this would be merely a waste of paper. What I have to say has been drawn from many years of reading and thinking about Chaucer, and I cannot be sure of the ultimate origins of all my ideas.

I have used footnotes to indicate particular important indebtedness and, in many cases, to refer the reader to more detailed discussions of various points than I have room for here, but I am afraid I cannot claim that I have used them with entire consistency. Chaucer was a fairly prolific poet, but compared to the kind of writer with whom I generally concern myself—Dickens or Mark Twain, for example—the body of his work is small. Many matters must be discussed in one form or another by everybody who attempts to write about him, and many ideas must necessarily occur independently to different writers. I certainly do not claim to have read everything that has been written about Chaucer, but neither have I listed everything that I have read. Nor have I thought it necessary to give credit to an article published in, say, 1953 for expressing an idea something like one which I myself have had in mind since about 1930.

In referring to the work of my predecessors, I have often inevitably been obliged to indicate agreement or disagreement. Such a book as this could have been written in no other way. But I do not wish at any point to be understood to imply that now that Sir Oracle has spoken, there is nothing more to be said upon the subject. I am not in the propaganda business, and I am not conducting a campaign for or against any individual or school of interpretation. Whether I myself am either "right" or "original" does not greatly interest me; my sole concern is to discover and to state the truth about Chaucer. I am indebted to those from whom I dissent as well as to those with whom I agree; in some cases, indeed, the two are one and the same.

I have italicized *The Canterbury Tales, Troilus and Criseyde,* and *The Legend of Good Women* and used quotation marks for other Chaucer titles not only in my own text but in all quotations and references, regardless of what system the writer being cited might have employed. Quotations from Chaucer's own writings are documented wherever I thought it necessary to enable the interested reader to find them in context, but when the title of a tale or short poem is given in my text, the documentation is often omitted. I realize that not all readers will agree with either the general principle or with my every application of it, but to document all quotations would have caused the footnotes to crawl up uncomfortably close to the top of the page. My Chaucer text is always that of F. N. Robinson, *The Works of Geoffrey Chaucer*, "New Cambridge Edition" (Houghton Mifflin Company, 1957), by permission of, and arrangement with, the publishers.

Finally, it is a great pleasure to be able here to express my gratitude to Professor James Root Hulbert, a distinguished Chaucer scholar, once one of my teachers at the University of Chicago, now a fellow resident of the Bay State, for his very great kindness in reading my manuscript. But it must be understood that responsibility for the judgments and evaluations expressed is mine alone.

EDWARD WAGENKNECHT

West Newton, Mass.
February 18, 1968

CONTENTS

xiii

The Personality of Chaucer

The following abbreviations are employed in footnotes:

"BD"	"The Book of the Duchess"
Col	Columbia University Press
CT	*The Canterbury Tales*
ELH	*English Literary History*
"HF"	"The House of Fame"
HM	Houghton Mifflin Company
HUP	Harvard University Press
JEGP	*Journal of English and Germanic Philology*
LGW	*The Legend of Good Women*
MLN	*Modern Language Notes*
MLQ	*Modern Language Quarterly*
MLR	*Modern Language Review*
MP	*Modern Philology*
OUP	Oxford University Press
"PF"	"The Parliament of Fowls"
PMLA	*Publications of the Modern Language Association*
PQ	*Philological Quarterly*
PUP	Princeton University Press
RES	*Review of English Studies*
SP	*Studies in Philology*
TC	*Troilus and Criseyde*

INTRODUCTION: CHAUCER
AND PSYCHOGRAPHY

> I have, God woot, a large feeld to ere,
> And wayke been the oxen in my plough.
>   "The Knight's Tale"

The latest and most authoritative collection of biographical
data about Chaucer[1] fills more than 600 large pages but con-
cerns itself largely with his official life;[2] for our understanding
of his character and personality we are, therefore, largely thrown
back upon the impressions we can derive from his own writings.
The question of how reliable these are for such a purpose must
therefore immediately be raised.

It has always been recognized that Chaucer was capable of
playing a roguish game of hide-and-seek with his readers and
often carrying it to the very verge of coyness, and that his com-

---

[1] *Chaucer Life Records*, edited by Martin C. Crow and Clair C. Olson, from
materials compiled by John M. Manly, Edith Rickert, and Lilian J. Redstone
(OUP, 1966). For Chaucerian backgrounds, see the same editors' *Chaucer's
World* (Col, 1948), made from materials gathered by Edith Rickert, and Roger
Sherman Loomis' more recent pictorial, *A Mirror of Chaucer's World* (PUP, 1965).

[2] James R. Hulbert, *Chaucer's Official Life* (Menasha, Wis. Banta, 1912).

ments, though abundant, are frequently noncommittal or patently ironical. Most scholars have always felt, nevertheless, that the man's personality did appear in his works; as C. E. Lawrence put it, Chaucer's readers "find themselves associated with a definite, a consistent, and a lovable being."[3] Not only does he join the pilgrims to Canterbury but he also introduces himself as a character in "The Book of the Duchess," "The House of Fame," "The Parliament of Fowls," and *The Legend of Good Women.* Even in *Troilus and Criseyde* he seems intent upon establishing a personal relationship at the outset, for he writes,

My purpos is, er that I parte fro ye . . . .

"Chaucer's personality," says J. S. P. Tatlock, "is one of the most marked and individual in literary history."[4]

Nowadays, however, it is not the fashion in literary scholarship to take anything that has hitherto seemed obvious for granted, and of late years a number of scholars have attempted to distinguish sharply between Chaucer himself and the "persona," as they are inclined to call it, who confronts us in *The Canterbury Tales* and elsewhere.[5] But in "The House of Fame" the narrator has

[3] "The Personality of Geoffrey Chaucer," *Quarterly Review,* Vol. CCXLII (1924), 315–33.

[4] *The Mind and Art of Chaucer* (Syracuse University Press, 1950).

[5] See E. Talbot Davidson, "Chaucer the Pilgrim," *PMLA,* Vol. LXIX (1954), 928–36, reprinted in Richard J. Shoeck and Jerome Taylor, eds., *Chaucer Criticism: The Canterbury Tales* (University of Notre Dame Press, 1960). See, further, Paul G. Ruggiers' sensible discussion of this matter in *The Art of the Canterbury Tales* (University of Wisconsin Press, 1965), 16ff., and, besides the references he gives, the following articles, expressing various points of view: Bertrand H. Bronson, "Chaucer's Art in Relation to His Audience," *University of California Publications in English,* Vol. VIII (1938), 1–53; Donald R. Howard, "Chaucer the Man," *PMLA,* Vol. LXXX (1965), 337–43; Robert M. Jordan, "The Narrator in Chaucer's *Troilus*," *ELH,* Vol. XXV (1958), 237–57; A. L. Kellogg, "Chaucer's Self-Portrait and Dante's" *Medium Aevum,* Vol. XXIX (1960), 119–20; Rosemary Woolf, "Chaucer as a Satirist in the General Prologue to the *Canterbury Tales,*" *Critical Review,* Vol. I (1959), 150–56. John M. Major, "The Personality of Chaucer the Pilgrim," *PMLA,* Vol. LXXV (1960), 160–62, examines Donaldson's criteria critically and unfavorably, and shows that if Chaucer did use a "persona" in *The Canterbury Tales,* he was no such simple soul as has been postulated by Donaldson, or, I might add, by Marchette Chute in her generally excellent biographical study, *Geoffrey Chaucer of England* (Dutton, 1946).

the Eagle call him "Geffrey" and refer to his official labors, while the Man of Law, in the Prologue to his tale, lists the writings of "Chaucer" and discusses their merits and demerits. It is difficult to see how the poet could have expected his readers to distinguish between such passages and others which he hypothetically did not intend to have applied to himself personally, and I myself can see no point in such supersubtle distinctions. "The 'I' in his poetry," says Bertrand H. Bronson bluntly, "never means anyone else than Geoffrey Chaucer, then and there visibly present," and Kemp Malone finds the writer plunging "into what amounts to a tête-à-tête with his readers" as early as the second metrical paragraph of the General Prologue to *The Canterbury Tales*. Since Chaucer was a writer of fiction, obviously some utterances were dramatic and must be understood to express the character rather than the author, but this much common sense has always understood, and in any case it is not the point under consideration here.

James Russell Lowell long ago denied Chaucer the dramatic gift, and the denial has recently been more dogmatically reaffirmed by D. W. Robertson, Jr.[6] But surely the Eagle, Criseyde, Pandarus, Harry Bailly, the Wife of Bath, the Pardoner, and the Friar in "The Summoner's Tale" are the greatest characters in English literature before Shakespeare, and surely Chaucer creates them as a dramatist would have created them by permitting them to talk themselves alive. Personally I have no more doubt that he would have written plays if he had lived in Elizabethan times than I can question that he would have been a novelist if he had been one of Queen Victoria's subjects, though I grant that he might have felt more at ease in the latter capacity; Kittredge was not the first reader who saw *Troilus and Criseyde* as a psychological novel. Scott, Dickens, Henry James, and a number of other masters have proved that the novelist is not debarred from using any of the dramatist's methods of creating character, but the dramatist *is* denied the privilege of direct comment which lies freely at the novelist's disposal, and this, I think, Chaucer might well have

[6] *A Preface to Chaucer* (PUP, 1962), 46ff.

found a deprivation.[7] C. N. Stavrou has remarked that "Chaucer could no more have taken himself seriously than Milton could have taken himself lightly,"[8] and I believe this to be true. Yet, though it would not be correct to say that he builds his work around his own personality as Milton does, it is not only because he is not writing plays that he gives us a more direct impression of himself than Shakespeare does. (Longfellow was not a dramatic poet, but he kept personalities out of his work almost as religiously as Browning did.) As we shall see later, even Chaucer's frequent self-depreciation (a stock device of humorists, including Mark Twain, for example) serves very effectively to keep him in the picture, and sometimes it leaves him in far more undisputed possession of the field than any amount of self-vaunting possibly could.

This is not to suggest that self-vaunting lay within Chaucer's range: I am sure that it did not. But I am also sure that it could never have occurred to him that it was necessary. And here, whatever may be thought of his dramatic power or the lack of it, he *is* like Shakespeare. He had Shakespeare's largeness and benignancy also and his capacity for accepting the universe: for all his surface irony and skepticism, his depths gravitated profoundly toward belief. We have more personal data for Shakespeare than we do for Chaucer, but here too we are thrown back upon inference from the work for most of what we think we know about the man's character, upon that and upon the impression that the *tone* of his writing makes upon us. In both cases it is well to be

---

[7] James B. Herrick, M.D., "Why I Read Chaucer at Seventy," *Annals of Medical History*, n.s. Vol. V (1933), 62–71, presents a nonspecialist's view, but such can be illuminating, especially when, as in this case, the writer is sensitive and learned in another field. Dr. Herrick finds of Chaucer that "he is ever present in his writings, whether he is telling a story, describing a scene, discoursing on astrology or predestination. His personality is not submerged or completely lost as is Shakespeare's. When Hamlet speaks it is Hamlet not Shakespeare who soliloquizes. When Palamon or Arcite or the Wife of Bath talk we realize that Chaucer is telling us what they say. And the marvel of it all is that we are not offended." I do not think the contrast is that sharp, and perhaps Herrick did not really think so either, for he added that Harry Bailly and the Wife of Bath "are as clear cut, as typical, as consistent, as Falstaff or Lady Macbeth."

[8] "Some Implications of Chaucer's Irony," *South Atlantic Quarterly*, Vol. LVI (1957), 454–61.

cautious about unverifiable assumptions, but a reasonable use of the imagination, informed by knowledge and guided by good judgment, is not to be denied, for there can be no scholarship of any depth without it; as Theodore Roosevelt once remarked, the use of the imagination makes for distortion in historical writing only when it is a distorted imagination. And it is as true in scholarship as it is in religion that while a reverent agnosticism may sometimes be fruitful, a blatant atheism can only make for sterility.

We may not know whether Shakespeare was a Catholic or a Protestant, whether he adored or despised Queen Elizabeth, or how happy he was with Anne Hathaway, but about what must have been the inner climate of Shakespeare's world we know a good deal. Ellen Terry once said she thought Shakespeare the only man she had ever really loved, and such sensitive readers as she do not make such remarks about writers whose work does not reveal them on a far deeper level than that which interests the readers of the gossip columns. If you think you do not know what Shakespeare was like, you might try to find out by asking yourself what he was *not* like. And do not stop with the primary-school questions, such as "Was Shakespeare like Hitler?" or even "Was Shakespeare like John Knox?" Move on to the college level and ask yourself, "Was Shakespeare like Dante? Milton? Dryden? Swift? Scott? Dickens?" (That he was not like Ben Jonson all the world has always known.) The answers will, I think, reflect varying shades of denial and affirmation, and neither could appear unless, in some measure, the writer's image had imprinted itself upon his work.

It is of course possible to reply to all this that even if we grant that Geoffrey Chaucer did present himself as the narrator of *The Canterbury Tales* and his other works, we still cannot be sure that the information he thus gives should be accepted at face value, since a writer's literary personality is not necessarily his "real" personality. Except that I should be slow to grant that the self which a poet expresses in his work is less "real" than the self he presents to the tax collector, I should freely admit this. As I hope I have already made clear, I am not claiming completeness,

7

finality, or inerrancy for the portrait of Chaucer contained in this volume. Only, I must insist that the distinction between literary personality and "real" personality, should you choose to make it, does not apply to Chaucer alone. It applies also to Dickens, Thackeray, William Faulkner, and him that died o' Wednesday, the only difference between Chaucer and these others being that with them we have an abundance of data from other sources with which we may compare and contrast the testimony of the works themselves. None of my readers can possibly lament the absence of such materials in Chaucer's case more than I do, but the difference between him and the others is still a difference in degree and not in kind. For if Chaucer used a "persona" in *The Canterbury Tales,* many of us do the same in our private correspondence, and I am not sure, dear reader, that you yourself are the same "persona" to all your correspondents, or that they all get the same impression of you. "All the world's a stage, and all the men and women merely players." Everybody's acting. No man reveals the whole of himself in his work, in his home, or in his play. The whole man must be sought in the sum of all these activities, but even when we have added them up, we can still miss the essence. Yes, even when we look within, the "persona" is still there, for who sees himself as he really is or could endure the sight? A French painter once declared that he could paint a dozen pictures of the same haystack, all different and all equally "true," but with no one of them exactly like the "real" haystack. The only truly "safe" psychographer, the only psychographer whose work can be accepted at face value, is God, and we are not gods but men. But being men, we must, in some measure, try to think God's thoughts after Him and trace the lines of His creation, and we must try to understand other men also. The Chaucer who appears in these pages is simply the Chaucer that the present writer has been able to grasp and to express in the light of the knowledge about him which now exists. If the reader can improve upon the picture, this will certainly be his own gain, and if he has the capacity to share his improvements with the world, it will mean gain for us all.

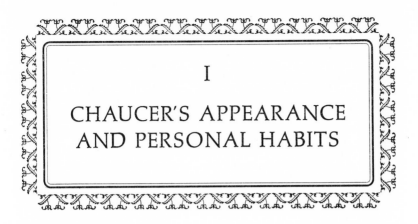

I
CHAUCER'S APPEARANCE AND PERSONAL HABITS

In the Prologue to his tale of "Sir Thopas" Chaucer is made the butt of one of Harry Bailly's rude but, in this case, good-natured jokes:

> "He in the waast is shape as wel as I;
> This were a popet in an arm t'embrace
> For any womman, smal and fair of face."

This is obviously a medieval version of "Nobody loves a fat man," and it would seem reinforced by the testimony of the portraits and by that of "Lenvoy de Chaucer a Scogan," to say nothing of the fact that Chaucer's bulk drove the Eagle who carried him to the House of Fame to profanity:

> "Seynte Marye!
> Thou art noyous for to carye."

What the beholder sees in the portraits must lie partly at least in the eye of the beholder, and nobody should be surprised that Lowell, who thought the Occleve portrait of Chaucer "more engaging than that of any other poet," should have seen more than most:

The downcast eyes, half sly, half meditative, the sensuous mouth, the broad brow, drooping with the weight of thought, and yet with an inexpungable youth shining out of it as from the morning forehead of a boy, are all noticeable, and not less so their harmony of placid tenderness. We are struck, too, with the smoothness of the face as of one who thought easily, whose phrase flowed naturally, and who had never puckered his brow over an unmanageable verse.[1]

This being his view, Lowell might well have disapproved of his publishers' choice of the Harvard portrait to illustrate his essay on Chaucer in the "Edition de Luxe" of his works, for Manly found here not the face of an old man but one that suggested "suffering and bad health."[2] The fair forked beard, the hooded eyes, the full lips, and a certain drooping which seems at once to suggest fatigue, irony, and good humor—this much is fairly evident to all of us in all the portraits.[3] That his height was about five feet six inches would seem to have been established in 1897 when his bones were exposed by the digging of Browning's grave in the Poets' Corner and measured by the coroner for Westminster.[4]

The Host also accuses Chaucer of being "elvyssh" (which, most likely, means abstracted, with a tendency toward mental absorption in matters not immediately at hand)[5] and of doing "daliaunce" to "no wight." This is on what is perhaps the second day of the pilgrimage, when he notices Chaucer for the first time,

> And seyde thus: "What man artow?" quod he;
> Thou lookest as thou woldest fynde an hare,
> For evere upon the ground I se thee stare."

[1] My Study Windows ("Chaucer").

[2] J. M. Manly, ed., The Canterbury Tales (Holt, 1928), 38.

[3] The fullest discussion of "The Portraits of Chaucer" is M. H. Spielmann's in Percy W. Ames, ed., Chaucer Memorial Lectures, 1900 (Asher & Co., 1900). Loomis' account in A Mirror of Chaucer's World is more recent and accessible.

[4] E. P. Hammond, Chaucer, A Bibliographical Manual, 47.

[5] See, for varying interpretations, T. A. Knott, "A Bit of Chaucer Mythology," MP, Vol. VIII (1910), 135–39; W. W. Lawrence, "Satire in 'Sir Thopas,'" PMLA, Vol. L (1935), 81–91; R. M. Lumiansky, "The Meaning of Chaucer's Prologue to 'Sir Thopas,'" PQ, Vol. XXVI (1947), 313–20.

Yet in the General Prologue Chaucer had represented himself as having spoken to all his fellow pilgrims at the Tabard Inn by nightfall of the first day, with the result

> That I was of hir felaweshipe anon.

If, as most of us are inclined to believe nowadays, Chaucer was born somewhere between 1343 and 1345, he was not an old man when he died in 1400[6] (Longfellow's reference to him as aged in the sonnet he wrote about him in 1875 is due to the fact that in those days he was generally believed to have been born in 1328), but since we do not know the cause of his death, we cannot tell whether the failure of his health was sudden or gradual. It would not appear that any man who pursued his very active career in the public service and managed to write a substantial amount of poetry besides could well have been sickly. Some have found a suggestion of weak eyes in the Eagle's

> "Thou sittest at another book
> Tyl fully daswed ys thy look,"

but this may seem a little strained; with fourteenth-century spectacles what they were, one would think that any eyes might become "daswed" if their owner read as much as Chaucer apparently did. In the Prologue to *The Legend of Good Women* there is an interesting incidental remark which may have some medical significance. Chaucer tells us how he returned from his worship of the daisy in the meadow and how, after his bed had been made up for him,

> I fel aslepe withinne an hour or two.

If this was his usual experience, he must have been at least a mild insomniac. There is nothing in the situation described which ought to have inspired sleeplessness in a person of normal habits, and the statement occurs in both versions of the Prologue. Would

---

[6] All we actually know about his age is that he must have been at least forty when he testified in the Scrope-Grosvenor case in 1386. The familiar 1340 was chosen for his birthdate only as a good round number.

a writer who was in the habit of falling alseep within a reasonable time after retiring express himself thus? I cannot answer the
question authoritatively, but it seems to me worth asking, and
my suspicions are reinforced when, at the beginning of the "Story"
part of "The House of Fame," Chaucer tells us that on one
particular occasion he "fil on slepe wonder sone." Unless this
was an unusual experience for him, where was the wonder?

As to Chaucer's personal habits, the Eagle's testimony is so
well-known that it hardly requires quotation:

> "thou hast no tydynges
> Of Loves folk yf they be glade,
> Ne of noght elles that God made;
> And noght oonly fro fer contree
> That ther no tydynge cometh to thee,
> But of thy verray neyghebores,
> That duellen almost at thy dores,
> Thou herist neyther that ne this;
> For whan thy labour doon al ys,
> And hast mad alle thy rekenynges,[7]
> In stede of reste and newe thynges,
> Thou goost hom to thy hous anoon;
> And, also domb as any stoon,
> Thou sittest at another book
> Tyl fully daswed ys thy look,
> And lyvest thus as an hermyte,
> Although thyn abstinence ys lyte,"[8]

Here is a charming picture of the devoted student, more interested in communing with his books in his study than in associating with his fellow men in the rude and vulgar world, and I do

---

[7] This is nearly always taken as a reference to Chaucer's labors in the customs.

[8] The "abstinence" or lack of it probably has nothing to do with sex. It is much
more likely to refer to indulgence in the pleasures of the table, probably with another side glance at Chaucer's weight. The portrait of the Franklin would seem to
reflect interest in good food, and Chaucer's treatment of the Cook very likely indicates that he was fastidious about it. The touch about the flies (*CT*, I, l. 4352)
is particularly interesting because in Chaucer's time nobody knew that flies near
food could endanger health.

not doubt that, as far as it goes, the picture is true. In most matters of temperament, Geoffrey Chaucer was not much like the Clerk of *The Canterbury Tales*—he certainly was no such innocent—but in their devotion to letters they were as one.

Yet Chaucer was not a professional scholar, nor even, as we now understand the term, a professional writer, and in view of the offices he held and the numerous diplomatic missions he undertook in the course of his career, it would be absurd to pretend that he was a shy man. I am not sure that his friendliness in the General Prologue is quite irreconcilable with the testimony of either Harry Bailly or the Eagle, but I think it best to postpone the discussion of this matter until a later stage of our inquiry.

II

CHAUCER'S BACKGROUND AND INTERESTS

Chaucer's background and his interests shade into each other imperceptibly, like those of any man. I shall consider backgrounds first, remembering always that my object is not to describe any of these things for their own sake but simply for the light they may shed upon his character and personality.

He spent his life in the public service, and though he was not a man of rank himself and had no member of the nobility among the Canterbury pilgrims, he associated with noble and even royal personages, and much of his income stemmed from the Crown. It seems that his wife Philippa had even closer ties with the court circle than he had and that his marriage to her may have contributed to his advancement. When, in 1386, she was received into the fraternity of Lincoln Cathedral, along with the future King Henry IV and others, she was the only woman in the company. But Chaucer had his place at court, and in the service of Elizabeth de Burgh, Countess of Ulster, and John of Gaunt, Duke of Lancaster and son of King Edward III, long before he married her, and if this had not been the case, it is hard to see how the marriage could have taken place. Even so, if Philippa was, as is now generally assumed, Philippa Roet, sister of Katherine Swynford, mistress and later third wife of John of Gaunt, she married somewhat "beneath" her. The Chaucer family hailed from Ipswich, and several names seem to have been attached to it. The one which stuck was apparently a trade-name, meaning "shoemaker" or "stocking-maker," but the trade by which we know the family best is that of vintner. There seems to have been considerable money. John Chaucer, the poet's father, was in the king's service before his son, and if the poet's public career was more important than that of his father, it was overshadowed in turn by that of his presumed son Thomas, who was a great man in the early fifteenth century. Geoffrey Chaucer was, in the course of his life, among other things, controller of the customs and subsidy of wools, skins, and hides for the Port of London (which was one of the king's principal sources of revenue), and later also of the petty customs on wine and other merchandise, clerk of the king's works, deputy forester in Somerset, knight of the shire and justice of the peace in Kent. As for the diplomatic missions in which he was engaged, though not all would go so far as E. P. Kuhl did when he called him "a towering public personage," he did go to the Continent a number of times in the company of important men who were engaged in the negotiation of important public business.[1]

In his writings the courtly atmosphere is all-pervasive, and we do not need the Cambridge manuscript miniature which shows him reading the *Troilus* before King Richard II[2] to be sure that Chaucer wrote for an aristocratic and exclusive circle. The circumstances under which he is believed to have written "The Book of the Duchess," "The House of Fame," "The Complaint of Mars," and *The Legend of Good Women* abundantly testify to his standing as a court poet, and the existence of rival theories of interpretation does not cancel out the court connection. Open Chaucer's poems almost at random and courtly and aristocratic

[1] Kuhl, "Chaucer the Patriot," *PQ*, Vol. XXV (1946), 277–80. See also Margaret Galway, "Geoffrey Chaucer, J.P. and M.P.," *MLR*, Vol. XXXVI (1941), 1–26.

[2] See Item #68 in Loomis, *A Mirror of Chaucer's World*.

references and interests will stare out at you: see the Prologue
to the *Legend* with its allusions to the flower and leaf cult and
the command that the commissioned work be presented to the
Queen at Eltham or at Shene; the allusion to the king's fool in
the *Troilus*;[3] the description of the heralds, their costumes, and
their coats of arms in "The House of Fame"[4] and the use of
"oundy," a technical term from heraldry, in the same poem;[5] the
description of the Squire in *The Canterbury Tales* with his
courtly accomplishments of riding, jousting, composing songs and
writing verses, drawing, singing, and fluting; the allusions to
courtly dancing in "The Franklin's Tale"[6] and "The House of
Fame";[7] and the incidental mention of the chivalric "champioun"
which Chaucer added to "The Man of Law's Tale."[8] When he
tells us of the Prioress that she

> peyned hire to countrefete cheere
> Of court,

he assumes that both he and his readers know the difference between the real and the counterfeit, just as clearly as his statement that she spoke French

> ful faire and fetisly,
> After the scole of Stratford atte Bowe,

assumes a knowledge of Parisian French. Properly speaking, Chaucer never had a "patron," though many writers have bestowed
that term upon John of Gaunt, from whom he derived income
for services rendered, and it is possible that the puzzling close
of "The Parliament of Fowls" may not be a bid for patronage.
But we shall still have "The Complaint of Chaucer to His Purse,"
with the lenvoy addressed to King Henry IV and hastily sent to
him after his accession, with highly satisfactory results, and this

[3] II, l. 400.
[4] Ll. 1320–40.
[5] L. 1386.
[6] *CT*, V, l. 918.
[7] Ll. 1235–36.
[8] *CT*, II, ll. 631–37.

16

shows that Chaucer remained a member of the court circle and behaved like a courtier to the very end of his days.

I have already indicated that Chaucer and wealth were not total strangers. The names of fine jewels and rare foods come readily to his mind—"swannes" and "heronsewes," for example, in the brief description of the feast in "The Squire's Tale"—and Chauntecleer's body is compared ironically to coral, jet, azure, and burnished gold. Of course a poet may write about wealth without having experienced it, and we may discount many passages, like the elaborate description of the Hall of Fame, with its gold plating, studded with bosses of fine fair stones, and the description of Fame's throne, formed like a great carbuncle, for almost anyone would furnish a rich setting here. But there are other passages which may possibly have some significance. In "The Book of the Duchess" Chaucer places himself in a rich setting. Here he wakes up in a luxurious chamber, with glazed windows and paintings:

> with glas
> Were al the wyndowes wel yglased,
> Ful clere, and nat an hoole ycrased.

When he suggests that there was "nat an hoole ycrased," is he suggesting that he was not quite used to such luxury, or might this have been the reaction of even a rich man in his time? I do not know. But both the *Legend* and the "Duchess" suggest that Chaucer was accustomed to personal servants.

> I bad men shulde me my couche make.[9]

> Upon my bed I sat upright
> And bad oon reche me a book.[10]

I do not believe that a man who was not accustomed to being waited on should put it that way, though of course that kind of personal service did not require great means in fourteenth-century England nor for a long time afterwards.

On the other hand, Chaucer knows the village and the country-

[9] G, l. 99.
[10] Ll. 46–47.

side quite as well as the court. He has seen "thise holtes" and "thise hayis" reclothe themselves in green after the long hard winter;[11] he has seen the falling oak,[12] the rooks' nests in the trees,[13] and the "mast" on which swine are fattened.[14] He speaks of corn in granges[15] and of sheaves in the barn.[16] He compares both the Greek host[17] and Fame's petitioners[18] to a swarm of bees, and he has studied the ever-widening circles which a stone creates when it is dropped into a pond.[19] He has apparently watched balky horses with the same amused tolerance with which he watched everything else, and fortunately for the readers of *Troilus and Criseyde*, he thought it worth while to try to understand "Bayard's" mental processes.[20]

Was this all observation, or did some experience enter into it? It is obviously difficult to tell where the line should be drawn. Certainly the observation cannot have been merely casual or superficial; without an intimate knowledge of town and country life Chaucer could hardly have written the fabliau tales. It was not the courtier who wrote of the Knight's Yeoman that

> His arwes drouped noght with fetheres lowe,

nor was it the courtier who described the

> many flowte and liltyng horn,
> And pipes made of grene corn,
> As han thise lytel herde-gromes,
> That kepen bestis in the bromes.[21]

Both the description in "The Reeve's Tale" of the miller who could fish and mend nets and turn cups on a lathe and the por-

[11] *TC*, III, ll. 351–57.
[12] *TC*, III, ll. 1380–83.
[13] "HF," l. 1516; *TC*, II, l. 1384.
[14] "HF," l. 1777.
[15] "HF," l. 698.
[16] "HF," l. 2140.
[17] *TC*, II, ll. 193–94.
[18] "HF," ll. 1520–25.
[19] "HF," ll. 788–803.
[20] *TC*, I, ll. 218–24.
[21] "HF," ll. 1223–26.

trait of the Reeve in the Canterbury *Prologue* suggest intimate knowledge of country life.[22]

But his background was wider yet. Even if you read only the General Prologue, you may be surprised by the breadth of his references. Not much can be claimed for his Craftsmen, but the Merchant's portrait shows knowledge, and the sketch of the Man of Law is full of technical terms.[23] The Shipman's "herberwe" and "lodemenage" are mentioned. Knowledge of the sea is suggested also in "Anelida and Arcite," where man's constancy is compared to a rotten mast in a tempest, and in the lively decription of the sea fight in the Cleopatra legend. Mention may be made also of Chaucer's references to land warfare, to the "pelet out of gonne"[24] and the stone shot from an engine.[25] In *Troilus and Criseyde* there is an interesting reference to them "that smale selys grave."[26] Apparently as Chaucer was familiar with all types and conditions of men, so he also knew something about everything from sea-fighting to seal-engraving. And with this we may well shift our emphasis from background to interests.[27]

We generally take it for granted that love of nature, as we understand it today, began with the Romantic Movement, but it

[22] Charles Muscatine comments, in D. S. Brewer's *Chaucer and Chaucerians* (University of Alabama Press, 1966), pp. 91–92, on Chaucer's similes involving common life: "Many of these comparisons are conventional, and many . . . are poetically just the right images in their contexts. Yet their number and their general character remain significant, especially as many come in poems and passages whose dominant associations are far from village and farm."

[23] In "Was Chaucer a Student at the Inner Temple?" in *The Manly Anniversary Studies* (University of Chicago Press, 1923), Edith Rickert restated the case for answering the question posed in her title in the affirmative. This resulted in a very general acceptance of an old tradition which scholars thought they had discarded. The only important skeptic is D. S. Bland, "Chaucer and the Inns of Court: A Re-examination," *English Studies*, Vol. XXXIII (1952), 145–55. Chaucer need not necessarily have studied law because he studied at the Temple. But legal knowledge would have been very useful, if not indispensable, to him in some of the posts he held. For Chaucer's education in general, see George A. Plimpton, *The Education of Chaucer* (OUP, 1935).

[24] "HF," l. 1643.

[25] "HF," ll. 1933–34.

[26] *TC*, III, l. 1462.

[27] With the conspicuous exception of F. N. Robinson, it seems to me that Chaucer scholars have treated Manly's tentative identification of a number of

is hard to see how any man could ever have loved nature more than Chaucer did. This was a full-grown interest in "The Book of the Duchess," and it had lost none of its charm when the time came to write *The Canterbury Tales.* As I have already suggested, many passages betray the close and careful observer. But Chaucer has never been loved primarily for his knowledge. He is loved for his enthusiasms, and there is no subject which more readily moved his enthusiasm than spring.

One or two passages out of many may be trusted to give the flavor. In the *Legend* Prologue he writes:

> whan that the month of May
> Is comen, and that I here the foules synge,
> And that the floures gynnen for to sprynge,
> Farewel my bok, and my devocioun!

In "The Knight's Tale" he adds to Boccaccio a passage in praise of May:

> "May, with alle thy floures and thy grene,
> Welcome be thou, faire, fresshe May,
> In hope that I some grene gete may."

And, of course, it has always been recognized that the opening lines of the General Prologue have as much of the spirit of spring in them as has ever been caught in any poem of the world.

For all that, Chaucer was not a "Romantic" poet. Bertrand H. Bronson has noted[28] that there is not a single visual image in the passage to which I have just referred and that Chaucer never looks to nature as a source for religious impulses and beliefs. To him, as to Dorigen in "The Franklin's Tale," the black rocks

---

originals for the Canterbury pilgrims (*Some New Light on Chaucer*) with more skepticism than it deserves. Kemp Malone, for example, *Chapters on Chaucer* (Johns Hopkins Press, 1951), Chapter X, hammers home the point that though the Host bears the name of an actual Harry Bailly, he is still a character of fiction and not a real person. This is incontestable, and in a world where people in general do not understand that there is a difference between art and life, the point is worth making, but it loses none of its validity if every one of Manly's originals is accepted, for Manly only suggested that actual persons had furnished Chaucer with material.

[28] *In Search of Chaucer* (University of Toronto Press, 1960).

off the coast of Brittany were horrible and dangerous and not in the least "picturesque," and though winter evening gave him one of his magical couplets in the portrait of the Friar—

> His eyen twynkled in his heed aryght,
> As doon the sterres in the frosty nyght—

he generally confines his appreciation to the amiable aspects of nature. He never makes nature his principal subject either, for he writes about men and women. But he does place them against a nature background, and this often contributes much of both atmosphere and understanding; how much more "unpleasant" would "The Merchant's Tale" be if its final scene took place in a bedchamber rather than in Januarie's garden! Winter was far more confining in the Middle Ages than it is now, and it is hard for us to realize the sense of liberation which the coming of spring must then have brought. Chaucer was "traditional" or "conventional" in his treatment of nature, but though it may be hard for moderns to realize it, a "conventional" reaction may be quite as "sincere" as an "unconventional" one. Thus the mere existence of a daisy cult at the English court does not prove that Chaucer did not love daisies, though I am afraid we can never be sure that he would have singled out that particular flower for praise if the cult had not been.

A very important element in the charm that spring held for Chaucer was furnished by the birds. He mentions many varieties. When Sir Thopas rides in the forest,

> The briddes synge, it is no nay,
> The sparhauk and the papejay,
>   That joye was to heere;
> The thrustlecok made eek his lay,
> The wodedowve upon the spray
>   She sang ful loude and cleere.

And when Criseyde surrenders to Troilus,

> as the newe abaysed nyghtyngale,
> That stynteth first whan she bygynneth to synge,

21

> Whan that she hereth any herde tale,
> Or in the hegges any wyght stirynge,
> And after siker doth hire vois out rynge,
> Right so Criseyde, whan hire drede stente,
> Opned hire herte, and tolde hym hire entente.[29]

Eagles are important in different ways in "The House of Fame" and "The Parliament of Fowls" (though Chaucer disclaims technical knowledge of eagles and of everything else), and in "The Parliament" the whole feathered kingdom is divided under four heads: birds of prey, worm-eaters, water-fowl, and seed-fowl.

More than one passage makes it clear that Chaucer passionately enjoyed the singing of birds. In "The Parliament" he writes,

> On every bow the bryddes herde I synge,
> With voys of aungel in here armonye.

In *Troilus and Criseyde* a nightingale sings the heroine to sleep:

> A nyghtyngale, upon a cedir grene,
> Under the chambre wal ther as she ley,
> Ful loude song ayein the moone shene,
> Peraunter, in his briddes wise, a lay
> Of love, that made hire herte fressh and gay,
> That herkned she so longe in good entente,
> Til at the laste the dede slep hire hente.[30]

And in "The Book of the Duchess" one would almost think Chaucer were describing a human choir:

> Me thoghte thus: that hyt was May,
> And in the dawenynge I lay
> (Me mette thus) in my bed al naked,
> And loked forth, for I was waked
> With smale foules a gret hep
> That had affrayed me out of my slep,
> Thorgh noyse and swetnesse of her song,
> And, as me mette, they sate among

[29] *TC*, III, ll. 1233–39.   [30] *TC*, II, ll. 918–24.

Upon my chambre roof wythoute,
Upon the tyles, overal aboute,
And songen, everych in hys wyse,
The moste solempne servise
By noote, that ever man, y trowe,
Had herde; for some of hem song lowe,
Som high, and al of oon accord.
To telle shortly, att oo word.
Was never herd so swete a steven,—
But hyt had be a thyng of heven.

Fur gets less attention than feathers. The rascally Friar in "The Summoner's Tale" (no cat-lover, he!) rudely brushes the cat off the bench before he sits down ("we know without need of more words," says Lowell, "that he has chosen the snuggest corner"). About the only gracious thing we know about "hende Nicholas" in "The Miller's Tale" is that he had a hole in his chamber door,

Ther as the cat was wont in for to crepe.

But Chaucer still thinks of the cat as a wild and mysterious animal, who cannot be tamed, and in whose breast the passion for the chase exceeds all others, and he permits the Wife of Bath, in her Prologue, to speak of an old superstition about singeing the cat's skin:

"Thou seydest this, that I was lyk a cat;
For whoso wolde senge a cattes skyn,
Thanne wolde the cat wel dwellen in his in;
And if the cattes skyn be slyk and gay,
She wol nat dwelle in house half a day,
But forth she wole, er any day be dawed,
To shewe hir skyn, and goon a-caterwawed."

Dogs fare somewhat better. In "The Merchant's Tale," Damyan, having won the favor of May, comes to Januarie

as lowe
As evere dide a dogge for the bowe.

More significant is a passage in "The Book of the Duchess," where a whelp which had followed the hunt comes to the dreamer and creeps as low as if it had known him,

> Helde doun hys hed and joyned hys eres,
> And leyde al smothe doun hys heres.
> I wolde have kaught hyt, and anoon
> Hyt fledde, and was from me goon;
> And I hym folwed. . . .

This sounds much like a true dog-lover. And Edwin J. Howard comments:

> Following the fleeing whelp is a highly realistic detail; it was always the duty of anyone on a hunt to capture any young dogs that strayed from the main pack. There is a fine artistry about this little episode; Chaucer uses the straying whelp to effect a smooth transition from the preliminary matter of the poem into his main theme. The device of the dog may also be found in French literature, but nowhere will one find such a genuine little whelp.[31]

Chaucer added squirrels to the list of animals that he found in the *Teseide* and took over into "The Parliament," and in "The House of Fame" he refers to the grimaces of apes. I have already spoken of horses and of bees. Snakes are mentioned only in the Cleopatra legend, where the queen dies the most horrible death that has ever been devised for her in a serpent pit. This seems to be peculiar to Chaucer and Gower (*Confessio Amantis*), and, as D. D. Griffith has remarked,[32] was probably suggested by the torments of Christian martyrs. Chaucer often compares the actions and aspects of human beings to those of animals. Sometimes, as in the description of Alison in "The Miller's Tale," this is done to secure a special effect, but he does it elsewhere also. It shows

---

[31] *Geoffrey Chaucer* (Twayne, 1964), 59.

[32] "An Interpretation of Chaucer's *Legend of Good Women*," in *The Manly Anniversary Studies*; reprinted in Edward Wagenknecht, ed., *Chaucer: Modern Essays in Criticism* (OUP, 1959).

24

close observation of animals and a certain amount of interest on his part.[33]

He says surprisingly little about trees; the only passage which comes readily to mind is the conventional allegorical one in "The Parliament of Fowls," in which many varieties are shown growing side by side. Gardens are another matter. There are the park "walled with grene ston" in the "Parliament," the "lytel herber that I have" in the *Legend*, and the gardens of Dorigen and of Januarie in *The Canterbury Tales*. In the former,

> They goon and pleye hem al the longe day.
> And this was on the sixte morwe of May,
> Which May hadde peynted with his softe shoures
> This gardyn ful of leves and of floures;
> And craft of mannes hand so curiously
> Arrayed hadde this gardyn trewely,
> That nevere was ther gardyn of swich prys,
> But if it were the verray paradys.

As for Januarie,

> He made a gardyn, walled al with stoon;
> So fair a gardyn woot I nowher noon.
> For, out of doute, I verraily suppose
> That he that wroot the Romance of the Rose
> Never koude of it the beautee wel devyse;
> Ne Priapus ne myghte nat suffise,
> Though he be god of gardyns, for to telle
> The beautee of the gardyn and the welle,
> That stood under a laurer alwey grene.

Equally charming is the garden in which Criseyde walks:

> This yerd was large, and rayled all th' aleyes,
> And shadewed wel with blosmy bowes grene,

[33] Beryl Raymond, "Aspects of Chaucer's Use of Animals," *Archiv*, Vol. CCI (1964), 110–14, observes, with much supporting evidence, that Chaucer used "simple and conventional ideas about animals to throw light on man," but did it with great skill and subtlety. On horses, see A. A. Dent, "Chaucer and the Horse," *Proceedings of the Leeds Philosophical and Literary Society*, Vol. IX (1959), 1–12.

And benched newe, and sonded alle the weyes,
In which she walketh arm in arm bitwene.

Those who know Chaucer best and value him most for his later, more realistic stories are always inclined to be surprised when they find him making use of "unnatural natural history." But among the birds in the "Parliament" we have the swan who sings at his death (who reappears at the end of the Dido legend), the owl who forebodes death, the scornful jay, the starling which betrays secrets, the faithful turtledove, and the stork who avenges adultery. Beryl Raymond, who has studied this topic most closely, finds that

> Chaucer's use of specific detail from the unnatural history of animals is small. Influential as the pseudo-scientific accounts of animals were in fixing the nature of beasts and in causing many curious ideas to be commonly accepted, Chaucer appears to have taken little interest in them. He seems to have been content to accept and to use the popular attributes of animals which were already part of folk belief.[34]

His temperament being what it was, Chaucer's partiality for nature is not hard to understand. If any English poet faces life unashamed, surely it is he. The passage in "The Manciple's Tale" in which, taking bird, cat, and wolf as illustrations, he sets out to demonstrate that

> ther may no man embrace
> As to destreyne a thyng which that nature
> Hath natureelly set in a creature

is compounded of Boethius and *The Romance of the Rose* but its spirit is Chaucer's. He was a child of Mother Earth, and he never felt disposed to disown her.

In Chaucer's time the English were an outdoor people, and we ought not to be surprised to find many references to hunting,

---

[34] "Chaucer and the Unnatural History of Animals," *Mediaeval Studies*, Vol. XXV (1963), 367–72.

fishing, and other outdoor sports in his poetry. G. G. Coulton felt that as a boy

> he played with other boys at forbidden games of ball in the narrow streets, to the serious risk of other people's windows or limbs; no doubt he brought his cock to fight in school under magisterial supervision, on Shrove Tuesday, and played in the fields outside the walls at the still rougher game of football, or at "leaping, dancing, shooting, wrestling, and casting the stone." In winter, when the great swamp of Moorfields was frozen, he would be sure to flock out with the rest to "play upon the ice. . . ."[35]

All this is as it may be; without "no doubt" every biographer would be out of business. But at least we may say that Chaucer grew up in a world in which this kind of thing was taking place. As to fish, I would conjecture that he liked both to look at them and to eat them, but whether he enjoyed catching them also, I have no idea. The "Parliament" garden has

> . . . colde welle-stremes, nothyng dede,
> That swymmen ful of smale fishes lighte,
> With fynnes rede and skales sylver bryghte,

and Januarie mentions both pickerel and pike, giving the preference to the former. There are certain specific references to particular methods of fishing also. Pandarus speaks of catching fish with nets,[36] and killing eels by stamping on them is mentioned in "The House of Fame."[37] "The Complaint of Mars" has a more interesting reference to fishing, however, not only because it is more detailed but because Chaucer succeeds for a moment in viewing the situation through the eyes of the fish:

> Hit semeth he hath to lovers enmyte,
> And lyk a fissher, as men alday may se,

---

[35] *Chaucer and His England* (Dutton, n.d.), 17–18.
[36] *TC*, II, l. 583.
[37] "HF," l. 2154. Cf. Robinson's note, *The Works of Geoffrey Chaucer*, p. 788. For other less significant references to fishing, see *TC*, II, l. 328–29 and III, l. 35.

> Baiteth hys angle-hok with some plesaunce,
> Til many a fissh ys wod til that he be
> Sesed therewith: and then at erst hath he
> Al his desir, and therewith al myschaunce;
> And thogh the lyne breke, he hath penaunce;
> For with the hok he wounded is so sore
> That he his wages hath for evermore.[38]

The hawk is an important character in the unfinished "Squire's Tale" and comes in elsewhere for brief though frequent mention. Sometimes technical terms are employed:

> Therfore, right as an hauk up at a sours
> Up springeth into th'eir . . .[39]

"Sours" occurs also in "The House of Fame,"[40] and "tulle," meaning "allure," is used in "The Reeve's Tale."[41] In *Troilus and Criseyde* we read of a sparhawk who has captured a lark, and the heroine herself appears before us

> As fresh as faukoun comen out of muwe.[42]

Even the Wife of Bath knows that

> With empty hand men may none haukes lure.[43]

Theseus in "The Knight's Tale" is a mighty hunter—

> For after Mars he serveth now Dyane—

and when Troilus is neither busy in bed nor slaughtering Greeks,

> on haukyng wolde he ride,
> Or elles honte boor, beer, or lyoun.[44]

Chaucer adds,

> The smale bestes leet he gon biside.

[38] Ll. 236–44.
[39] *CT*, III, ll. 1938–39.
[40] L. 551.
[41] *CT*, I, l. 4134.
[42] III, ll. 1191–92, 1784.
[43] *CT*, III, l. 415.
[44] *TC*, III, ll. 1779–80.

Let us hope they appreciated it. It was more than Sir Thopas did for them, for he is sarcastically described as going out after mighty game, "bothe bukke and hare." There are many hunting pictures in the magician's revelations to Aurelius in "The Franklin's Tale," and everybody remembers the Monk of the General Prologue:

> Grehoundes he hadde as swift as fowel in flight;
> Of prikyng and of hunting for the hare
> Was al his lust, for no cost wolde he spare.

Somewhat more significant is the description of the hunt in "The Book of the Duchess," for here a number of technical terms are employed: "foresters," "relayes" (reserve packs of hounds), "lymeres" (hounds held in leash), and "founes, sowres, bukkes" (deer one, four, and six years old respectively). These lines clearly come from experience:

> The houndes had overshote hym alle,
> And were on a defaute yfalle.
> Therwyth the hunte wonder faste
> Blew a forloyn at the laste.[45]

Yet I am by no means sure that Chaucer was a hunter. Oliver Farrar Emerson, who made the most elaborate study we have of "Chaucer and Mediaeval Hunting,"[46] believed that "Chaucer knew much more mediaeval hunting practice than has usually been supposed." But it was the way of writers like Chaucer and Shakespeare to give the impression that they knew all about everything, and they cannot possibly have experienced everything. In the *Legend* Prologue the birdcatcher is described as

> The foule cherl that for his coveytyse
> Hadde hem betrayed with his sophistrye.

Kemp Malone seems to think it significant that Chaucer cut the

[45] Ll. 383–86. See, further, *CT*, VII, ll. 110–11 and *TC*, II, l. 966, with Robinson's note.
[46] *Romantic Review*, Vol. XIII (1922), 115–50; reprinted in Emerson's *Chaucer Essays and Studies* (Western Reserve University Press, 1929).

hunting scene in "The Book of the Duchess" short—only forty-three lines—and draws the conclusion that "he had no special interest in hunting as a literary theme." He does say, "I was ryght glad" when he hears the horns of the hunters, but this might be discounted as a conventional device for drawing the dreamer into the hunt and the ensuing encounter with the Black Knight. Walter in "The Clerk's Tale" is blamed not for hunting per se but for devoting himself to it to the neglect of his duties as a ruler.[47] Emily's devotion to hunting in "The Knight's Tale" and her desire to give herself to the chase rather than to marriage may merely indicate her devotion to Diana; we never see her at the hunt. On the other hand, there can be no question about Dido's blood-lust in the Legend, and Chaucer does not seem less sympathetic toward her on this account.

Wrestling and archery are mentioned also. The government encouraged the latter out of consideration for what is euphemistically denominated "national defence," even when frowning on other dangerous sports. The Miller of The Canterbury Tales was a good wrestler, and so was Sir Thopas, who was also an archer.

> Therto he was a good archeer;
> Of wrastlyng was ther noon his peer,
> Ther any ram shal stonde.

Neither, of course, was a proper knightly exercise. But the attitude toward wrestling is obviously a detached one:

> For many a man that may nat stonde a pul,
> It liketh hym at the wrastlynge for to be.[48]

It is possible that Chaucer's bulk put him in this class, but the detachment may well apply to other sports also. Coulton observes that "however he may have revelled with the rest in his wilder

---

[47] "But, right as they were bounden to a stake" in "The Clerk's Tale," CT, IV, l. 704, has sometimes been taken as a reference to bearbaiting, but Manly (Canterbury Tales, p. 593) categorically denies this: "That was not the only purpose for which stakes were used."
[48] "PF," ll. 164–65.

youth, the elvish and retiring poet of the *Canterbury Tales* mentions the sports of the townsfolk only with gentle irony."

I should say much the same about games and indoor sports. Dice-playing is mentioned occasionally. From the Franklin's point of view, at least, it is a vice.[49] Chess and backgammon twice occur together,[50] and the Black Knight's description of the loss of his queen shows a knowledge of the game and of the terms used in connection with it. Even here, however, Chaucer's attitude seems slighting, and he takes pains to explain that it is better to read romances than to play chess or backgammon.

When we come to entertainment and the drama the situation is very different. "Hende Nicholas" in "The Miller's Tale," playing upon the Carpenter's credulity when trying to get him out of the way so that he may bed with his wife, refers to the well-known comedy treatment of Noah's wife in the mystery plays:

> "Hastou nat herd," quod Nicholas, "also
> The sorwe of Noe with his felaweshipe,
> Er that he myghte gete his wyf to shipe?"

Nicholas was something of an authority in this field, for he himself was an actor:

> Sometyme, to shewe his lightnesse and maistrye,
> He pleyeth Herodes upon a scaffold hye.

We may be sure that he played him as broadly as possible, and the Miller's Prologue is generally supposed to contain another reference to the rambunctious side of the mysteries, where it is recorded of the Miller himself that

> in Pilates voys he gan to crie.[51]

The Wife of Bath, too, enjoyed such entertainments, and in view

---

[49] *TC*, IV, l. 1098; *CT*, V, l. 900.
[50] "BD," l. 51; *CT*, V, l. 900.
[51] This has been questioned by Leonard Ellinwood, "A Further Note on 'Pilates Voys,'" *Speculum*, Vol. XXVI (1951), 482, where a musical interpretation is proposed. Cf. Roscoe E. Parker, " 'Pilates Voys,' " *Speculum*, Vol. XXV (1950), 237–44; Kelsie B. Harder, "Chaucer's Use of the Mystery Plays in 'The Miller's Tale,' " *MLQ*, Vol. XVII (1956), 193–98.

of her well-known fondness for being the center of attention, she might well have enjoyed appearing in them also had this been possible.

The drama was still in an embryonic form in Chaucer's time, but the court did not lack entertainment. The best passage is in "The House of Fame," lines 1182–1281, where we read of minstrels, harpers, pipers, jugglers, magicians, etc.

> Ther saugh I pleye jugelours,
> Magiciens, and tregetours,
> And Phitonesses, charmeresses,
> Olde wicches, sorceresses,
> That use exorsisacions,
> And eke these fumygacions;
> And clerkes eke, which konne wel
> Al this magik naturel,
> That craftely doon her ententes
> To make, in certeyn ascendentes,
> Ymages, lo, thrugh which magik
> To make a man ben hool or syk.

One of these illusionists Chaucer calls by name, and we now know that he spoke here of an actual contemporary:[52]

> Ther saugh I Colle tregetour
> Upon a table of scyamour
> Pleye an uncouth thyng to telle;
> Y saugh him carien a wynd-melle
> Under a walsh-note shale.

Similar feats are spoken of in "The Franklin's Tale," where of course, the story turns upon an illusionist's tricks:

> "For ofte at feestes have I wel herd seye
> That tregetours, withinne an halle large,
> Have maad come in a water and a barge,
> And in the halle rowen up an doun.

[52] James F. Royster, "Chaucer's 'Colle Tregetour,'" SP, Vol. XXIII (1926), 380–84.

> Sometyme hath semed come a grym leoun;
> And somtyme floures sprynge as in a mede;
> Somtyme a vyne, and grapes white and rede;
> Sometyme a castel, al of lym and stoon;
> And whan hem lyked, voided it anon.
> Thus semed it to every mannes sighte."

Now, of course, we are moving over into the world of the arts, where Chaucer's sympathies might reasonably be expected to be more deeply enlisted.

There have been few periods of history [writes Joan Evans authoritatively] in which the links between literature and decorative art were closer than in the fourteenth century. The transference of themes from Romance to tapestries, embroideries, goldsmith's work and ivories is a commonplace of artistic history; but in return certain poets—and Chaucer most of all—took themes from the decorative arts of their day and made them a part of their verse.[53]

The luxurious room in which the poet wakes up in "The Book of the Duchess" had the story of Troy in stained glass.

> And alle the walles with colours fyne
> Were peynted, both texte and glose,
> Of al the Romaunce of the Rose.

In the Temple of Brass in "The Parliament of Fowls" the walls were painted with scenes from classical stories, and there was a series of paintings illustrating the *Aeneid* in Venus' temple in "The House of Fame." A wealth of images appears in this poem:

> Yet sawgh I never such noblesse
> Of ymages, ne such richesse,
> As I saugh graven in this chirche.

Rich tabernacles, pinnacles, and quaint figures of goldwork are specifically mentioned. The Summoner's "fyr-reed cherubynnes face" probably derives from ecclesiastical art.

[53] "Chaucer and Decorative Art," *RES*, Vol. VI (1930), 408–12.

But all this evinces more knowledge than interest. How much Chaucer cared for painting, and what his personal tastes were, I have no idea. With certain modern calamities in mind it is tempting to read significance into

> "For if a peyntour wolde peynte a pyk
> With asses feet, and hede it as an ape,
> It cordeth naught, so nere it but a jape."[54]

But I fear that my reaction here stems from painful experience which Chaucer was spared. Though it would be reasonable to assume that the frequency with which he refers to paintings evidences some interest on his part, I must say that his references to the sense of smell—the comparison between the breath of Eolus' trumpet, for example, to

> a pot of bawme helde
> Among a basket ful of roses,[55]

and the mention elsewhere of "bawme . . . fletyng every mede" in spring—indicate far more sensitiveness in this direction than is anywhere indicated for art.

There is not much on architecture either. Chaucer knew that a good builder does not rush to work "with rakel hond,"[56] and that a strong house needs a strong foundation, but we all know that much. When he finds the House of Fame built upon ice, he exclaims:

> "By seynt Thomas of Kent!
> This were a feble fundement
> To bilden on a place hye.
> He ought him lytel glorifye
> That hereon bilt, God so me save!"

from which he goes on to describe the palace in some detail:

> Al was of ston of beryle,

[54] *TC*, II, ll. 1041–43.
[55] "HF," ll. 1685–86.
[56] *TC*, I, l. 1067.

> Bothe the castel and the tour,
> And eke the halle and every bour,
> Withouten peces of joynynges.
> But many subtil compassinges,
> Babewynnes and pynacles,
> Ymageries and tabernacles,
> I say; and ful eke of wyndowes,
> As flakes falle in grete snowes.

On the other hand, Chaucer shows great interest in music. He began with the music of nature—the sound of the wind in the leaves and the singing of the birds,

> For ther was noon of hem that feyned
> To synge, for ech of hem hym peyned
> To fynde out mery crafty notes.
> They ne spared not her throtes.[57]

From here he passed on to the music of man. He knows various types of instruments, classifying them in *Troilus and Criseyde* as wind, touch, and cord instruments.[58] His court experience has made him thoroughly familiar with harpers, and he mentions them on several occasions. He is also familiar with the use of music for exciting emotion, especially in warfare:

> Tho saugh I in an other place
> Stonden in a large space,
> Of hem that maken blody soun
> In trumpe, beme, and claryoun;
> For in fight and bloodshedynge
> Ys used gladly clarionynge.[59]

He bestows a pair of bagpipes on the Miller and makes Nicholas play "a gay sautrie," to which he sings "the Kynges Noote" and "*Angelus ad virginem.*" In "The Miller's Tale" also Absolon's music is closely associated with his dancing, which is described

[57] "BD," ll. 317–20.
[58] TC, V, ll. 442ff.
[59] "HF," ll. 1237–42.

satirically. Stringed instruments are described as of ravishing sweetness, quite in the modern manner:

> Of instruments of strenges in acord
> Herde I so pleye a ravyshyng swetnesse,
> That God, that makere is of al and lord,
> Ne herde nevere beter, as I gesse.[60]

Chaucer's familiarity with the great ecclesiastical music of his time is unquestionable, and his reference to the song of the Prioress as

> Entuned in hir nose ful semely

is probably not satirical but rather indicative of his knowledge that the recitative portions of the service were chanted in this way.[61]

Manly is the scholar who has gone farthest toward suggesting that since he began his poetic career in the school of Machaut, Chaucer may well have composed the music for many of his lost "balades, roundeles, vyrelayes," as well as writing the words.[62] Naturally we cannot be sure of this, but, as Manly says, "the marriage of verse to music was the very essence of the new technique," and the Squire of *The Canterbury Tales* is very carefully endowed with both gifts:

> He koude songes make and wel endite.

Clair C. Olson, on the other hand, views Chaucer's musical competence somewhat disparagingly. He thinks that Chaucer

> either did not know or did not care much about the theoretical aspects of music. His writings present us with a fairly representative, though not a complete, list of the instruments in use at the time, but he tells us very little about ensembles. He was interested in the numerous ways in which music of many kinds entered into the lives of all sorts of people in fourteenth-century England, and yet he tells us much more

[60] "PF," ll. 197–200.
[61] Manly, *CT*, p. 504.
[62] Manly, *Some New Light*, 278–79; *CT*, pp. 502–503.

about amateur musical performances than he does about the activities of professional minstrels.[63]

But is not this exactly what we might expect from the kind of writing Chaucer did? As for his "seeming preference for vocal rather than instrumental music," this would be quite natural in view of the comparatively undeveloped state of instrumental music in Chaucer's time, and it would also be characteristic of his concentration upon the direct expression of human personality in all areas of his interest. Moreover, he did not neglect instrumental music, and Olson's idea that he became less interested in music as he grew older is purely speculative.[64]

Tradition makes Chaucer a great and well-nigh universal scholar.

> Leland tells us that . . . [he] left the university an acute logi-
> cian, a delightful orator, an elegant poet, a profound philoso-
> pher, and an able mathematician. Not satisfied with this, he
> added the further statement that he was a devout theologian.
> These assertions were repeated by both Bale and Pitts.[65]

Modern commentators, perhaps overimpressed by the fact that they have been able to catch him in a number of errors, most of which are no more important than Shakespeare's ignorance of the fact that Bohemia lacked a seacoast, have often minimized his learning. Even if it is true that he had training in law, he cannot possibly have had an expert's knowledge in all the fields in which it has been credited to him, and we ought not to be greatly distressed if it should turn out that he got most of his knowledge of medicine from Vincent of Beauvais.[66] Highly specialized knowl-

---

[63] "Chaucer and the Music of the Fourteenth Century," *Speculum*, Vol. XVI (1941), 64-91.

[64] See further musical references in Muriel Bowden, *A Commentary on the General Prologue to* The Canterbury Tales (Macmillan, 1948), 89.

[65] Thomas Lounsbury, *Studies in Chaucer, His Life and Writings* (Harpers, 1891), I, 170.

[66] See Pauline Aiken, "Vincent of Beauvais and Dame Pertelote's Knowledge of Medicine," *Speculum*, Vol. X (1935), 281-87; "Arcite's Illness and Vincent of Beauvais," *PMLA*, Vol. LI (1936), 361-69; "The Summoner's Malady," *SP*, Vol. XXXIII (1936), 40-44.

edge on the part of a great creative writer seems quite as likely to spoil his work as to aid it, yet his own imagination often anticipates both scientific discovery and his own experience. When in "The House of Fame" the Eagle reveals an ambition to become an instructor in physics, telling Chaucer that words create in the atmosphere circles similar to those which appear in a pond when a stone is cast into it, the exposition closes with the words

"Take yt in ernest or in game."

Skeat preferred to "take yt in game,"[67] but Lowes, who finds "the scope of Chaucer's reading . . . as amazing as the range of his activities," calls it "a long and acute and surprisingly correct demonstration of the way in which sound travels through the air,"[68] and Manly, who, without foolishly pretending that Chaucer was a professional scholar, yet gives him credit for "scholarly tastes and . . . considerable erudition," comes about as close to asperity as he ever gets, when he goes on to remark that "there are few of his critics whose errors are less numerous than his."[69] And if the critics had to do their work with the equipment that was available to the poet we may reasonably suppose that their errors would be much more numerous than they are.

Chaucer was quite cognizant of the expansion of knowledge in his time, for he speaks of "al this newe science that men lere."[70] "The House of Fame" has a possible allusion to the magnifying glass,[71] and the magnet is referred to in the "Parliament."[72] In "The Book of the Duchess" the circulation of the blood was described long before Harvey:

The blood was fled for pure drede
Doun to hys herte, to make hym warm—
For wel hyt feled the herte had harm—

[67] Walter W. Skeat, ed., The Oxford Chaucer (OUP, 1894–97), III, 260.
[68] John Livingston Lowes, Geoffrey Chaucer and the Development of His Genius (HM, 1934), 113, 204.
[69] Chaucer and the Rhetoricians (OUP, 1926), reprinted in Shoeck and Taylor, eds., Chaucer Criticism, II (Notre Dame University Press, 1962).
[70] "PF," l. 25.
[71] L. 1290.
[72] Ll. 148ff.

> To wite eke why hyt was adrad
> By kynde, and for to make hyt glad;
> For hit is membre principal
> Of the body; and that made al
> Hys hewe chaunge and wexe grene
> And pale, for ther noo blood ys sene
> In no maner lym of hys.[73]

However and wherever he got it, Chaucer knew enough about medicine to list all the principal authorities known to the science of his time, and he knew medieval medical theory well enough to discuss "humors" and "hereos" and the causes of the Summoner's fire-red cherub's face. He knew that abuses exist in the medical profession as well as in the church, and he knew too that medieval remedies are not always pleasant—

> O, sooth is seyd, that heled for to be
> As of a fevre, or other gret siknesse,
> Men moste drynke, as men may ofte se,
> Ful bittre drynke—[74]

but he knew a great deal more than that. The diet of worms which that all-knowing, practical-minded domestic physician Pertelote prescribes for her lord in "The Nun's Priest's Tale" admirably suits Chaucer's satiric purpose in weaving back and forth between man and fowl, but he is not merely clowning: worms *were* used in the medieval pharmacopoeia.[75]

[73] Ll. 490–99.
[74] *TC*, III, ll. 1212–15.
[75] No reader of Chaucer should miss Walter Clyde Curry's fascinating book, *Chaucer and the Mediaeval Sciences* (OUP, 1926). In *Some New Light*, p. 226, Manly says that it seems to be Curry's view "that Chaucer's characters are not portraits drawn from life but artificial constructions from scientific data. Chaucer's point of departure for a portrait would be the scientific summary of the physical and psychological characteristics of a temperament or the features of physique, character, and incident determined by an astrological horoscope." This may be just in its application to Curry's early work, but in his book, published the same year as *Some New Light*, he specifically disavows it: "the present writer . . . once entertained the perilous theory that Chaucer may have fashioned Dame Alisoun in accordance with astrological principles. . . . But upon more mature consideration I have concluded that such a theory in application is so mechanical and so simple in its execution that

In "The House of Fame" the Eagle suggests only a literary reason why Chaucer should submit himself to him for a lesson in astronomy, and Chaucer declines on the very sensible ground that he can enjoy the authors who write about people who have been turned into constellations even though he is not able to locate the constellations themselves in the sky. Actually, however, he seems to have had considerable interest in astronomy for its own sake. No reader will need to be told that his poetry is crammed with astronomical allusions, and though there are different interpretations of the meaning of "The Complaint of Mars," that it is based on astronomical knowledge is not debatable. Like the Host before "The Man of Law's Tale," Chaucer's characters often use such knowledge for even so practical an operation as the determination of time.

> Our Hooste saugh weel that the brighte sonne
> The ark of his artificial day hath ronne
> The ferthe part, and half an houre and moore,
> And though he were nat depe ystert in loore,
> He wiste it was the eightetethe day
> Of Aprill, that is messager to May:
> And saugh wel that the shadwe of every tree
> Was as in lengthe the same quantitee
> That was the body erect that caused it.
> And therfore by the shadwe he took his wit
> That Phebus, which that shoon so clere and brighte,

---

the resultant figure is likely to be little better than a highly colored dummy galvanized into a semblance of activity and emotion by astral influences, and in no sense a complex human being. Under the spell of Chaucer's pen one rests under the illusion that the Wife of Bath is a complex human being. . . . I do not know how Chaucer has created such a character, but I suspect that the soul and personality of this woman was conceived in the poet's imagination as a complete whole. . . . In the process of creation the astrological material has played only a relatively small part. But a full interpretation of the horoscope and a consideration of astral influences moving upon the character in question would seem to be necessary for a thorough understanding of the poet's original conception." Curry's chapter on the Wife of Bath, one of his best, is reprinted in my *Chaucer: Modern Essays in Criticism.* There is, of course, no reason why a poet may not interpret even a character whose original he has observed in the light of the known or supposed knowledge of his day.

> Degrees was fyve and fourty clombe on highte;
> And for that day, as in that latitude,
> It was ten of the clokke, he gan conclude.

This is more than any modern "nat depe ystert in loore" could have achieved. But of course the most important single item is "A Treatise on the Astrolabe," written for "lyte Lowys my sone," which a high authority has described as "the oldest work written in English upon an elaborate scientific instrument,"[76] and if scholars finally decide that "The Equatorie of the Planets" is Chaucer's also, this will provide further evidence of very keen interest and considerable knowledge.[77]

Of course Chaucer did not always distinguish between astronomy and astrology so sharply as we do. He thinks of the nine spheres as the sources of music and melody, and the Franklin can hardly have been speaking for him when he said, "I ne kan no termes of astrologye." The clerk in "The Miller's Tale"

> Hadde lerned art, but al his fantasye
> Was turned for to lerne astrologye.

He was a weather prophet also, and Chaucer was familiar with his almageste, his astrolabe, and his augrim stones. The misfortunes of Constance, Criseyde, and many more were written in the stars:

> For in the sterres, clerer than is glas,
> Is writen, God woot, whoso koude it rede,
> The deeth of every man, withouten drede.[78]

Chaucer's Doctor casts horoscopes for his patients, and when Palamon and Arcite are in the depths of their troubles, Arcite exclaims,

[76] See Robinson, p. 545. Sister M. Madeleva's essay on the "Astrolabe"—"A Child's Book of Stars"—in her A Lost Language and Other Essays on Chaucer (Sheed and Ward, 1951) is one of the most charming pieces ever written about the poet. For a general study of the astronomical field, see Florence M. Grimm, "Astronomical Lore in Chaucer," University of Nebraska Studies in Language, Literature and Criticism, No. 2 (1919).

[77] See Robinson, pp. viii–ix; Howard, pp. 103–104.

[78] CT, II, ll. 194–96.

"So stood the hevene whan that we were born,
We moost endure it; this is the short and playn."

Even those who are not willing to go as far as Curry goes in at-
tributing the joys and woes of the Wife of Bath to astrological
influences must admit that astrology was in her mind and therefore in that of her creator:

The children of Mercurie and of Venus
Been in hir wyrkyng ful contrarius;
Mercurie loveth ryot and dispence.
And, for hire diverse disposicioun,
Ech falleth in otheres exaltacioun.
And thus, God woot, Mercurie is desolat
In Pisces, wher Venus is exaltat;
And Venus falleth ther Mercurie is reysed.[79]

Believers in astrology often believed in alchemy also. Besides
briefer references elsewhere, Chaucer discusses it at length in "The
Canon Yeoman's Tale," and the experts tell us that only one who
knew astrological terms and conceptions could have jumbled them
so artfully as he did to reveal the Yeoman's ignorance of the mysteries at which he assists. Perhaps the boldest of all Manly's bold
speculations, following H. G. Richardson's discoveries concerning
the alchemical practices of Canon William Shuchirch at Windsor,
was to the effect that Chaucer himself fell into the hands of the
alchemists in his later years, and that this explains the frequent
borrowings of money which have so puzzled his biographers. In
our present state of knowledge, it is difficult to be dogmatic as to
Chaucer's attitude toward alchemy, but he was certainly interested in the subject, and he may well have wavered in his views.
"The Parson's Tale" denounces all magic as irreligious, and this
is in harmony with the declaration in "The Franklin's Tale":

For hooly chirches feith in oure bileve
Ne suffreth noon illusioun us to greve.[80]

[79] CT, III, ll. 699–705.
[80] Manly, *Some New Light*, 242–48. S. Foster Damon, "Chaucer and Alchemy,"
PMLA, Vol. XXXIX (1924), 782–88, sees Chaucer as himself an adept, opposing

Of course the Middle Ages were also committed to physiognomy and a great many other, as we should say, pseudo-sciences: the Pardoner's hair, the Reeve's skinny legs, the Friar's soft neck, the wart on the Miller's nose, and many more details which to modern readers are only picturesque would have had significance for Chaucer's contemporaries.

"Dreams," wrote George Lyman Kittredge, "play as large a role in Chaucer as presentiments do in Shakespeare. We may guess, if we like, that Shakespeare was in his own person susceptible to presentiments and that Chaucer, for his part, had uncommonly vivid dreams."[81] Yes, we may certainly do this "if we like," but in Chaucer's case it would not be wise, for we should be ignoring the large conventional role that dreams play in the French vision poems which served as his models during the first part of his career. Chaucer may, as has been said, have had as much interest in dreams as Freud, but I think he would have refused to lie down in the bed of Procrustes which Freudian interpreters of dreams have prepared for us. The ideas expressed in the elaborate discussion of dreams at the beginning of "The House of Fame" may show Chaucer's own interest in the subject, but the ideas expressed are not original with him. In "The Nun's Priest's Tale," which is drenched in dream-lore, the skeptical and materially-minded Dame Pertelote is confounded by the event while the superstitious but more imaginative Chauntecleer is justified, but this may have been determined by the needs of the story and the writer's desire to satirize a "Martha"-type of woman. Pandarus is equally skeptical in *Troilus and Criseyde,* but on at least one occasion, Troilus, like Peter Ibbetson, "dreams true."[82]

More interesting than any of this to students of his art is the skill with which Chaucer uses dreams, even in his earliest work. "The Book of the Duchess" has more continuity than a real dream; otherwise it could not be a satisfying work of art. But there

only false alchemists. Like Manly, I do not find the argument convincing, and I may add that the reader would have to be an adept himself to understand the argument after reading Damon's article. On this whole matter, see also Mary Edith Thomas, *Medieval Skepticism and Chaucer* (William-Frederick Press, 1950), 111ff.

[81] *Chaucer and His Poetry* (HUP, 1915), 67.

[82] *TC,* V, ll. 358ff., 1238ff.

are touches which show clearly that Chaucer knew just what he was doing. The general atmosphere is not undreamlike; as Kittredge says, the mental attitude of the dreamer is throughout that of childlike wonder, and many readers who have been annoyed by what seems to them his inexplicable obtuseness would seem to have failed to take this sufficiently into account. The sudden intrusion of the Emperor Octavian into a place where nobody would expect to find him is a masterly touch; so is the way in which the little whelp disappears when he has served his function and, again, the way the story of the hunt leads, for no particular reason, to the Black Knight.[83] The dreamer's horse, too, suddenly disappears,

[83] It is generally taken for granted that Chaucer is the dreamer in "The Book of the Duchess" and that the Black Knight is John of Gaunt. When I first read the poem in 1923, I suggested the possibility that the Black Knight might be not John of Gaunt but Chaucer himself. The age of the Black Knight is given as twenty-four years. John of Gaunt was twenty-nine in 1369 when Blanche the duchess died. But if Chaucer was born in 1345, as he may have been, then his age would be just right. The Black Knight is a poet, and there is no record of John of Gaunt having made verses. In l. 37 Chaucer refers to his eight-year sickness, declares that only one physician could heal him, and then passes the matter over "until eft." If he does not return to this in the story of the Black Knight, then he does not return to it in the poem at all. Chaucer may have entered John of Gaunt's service in 1361, which would mean that he had been in the household just eight years when Blanche died, thus making his eight-year sickness the conventional devotion of the page to his mistress. This assumption would explain too the humility of the lover, the apparently higher rank of the lady, and the references to the various favors which she bestowed upon the knight. There is no indication of either betrothal or marriage at any point; in fact ll. 1271-72 seem definitely to rule sex out of their relationship. I am not prepared to go to the literary barricades to defend any of this, but it is interesting to see how many arguments can be invoked. When I expounded this theory to Edith Rickert, I became aware that the possibility had already occurred to her. She felt that the greatest weakness inherent in this interpretation was the necessity it would impose of believing that Chaucer appeared in the poem—and in the dream—in a double aspect, conversing with himself. An extensive course of reading in French vision poems might, she thought, show whether anything like this had occurred elsewhere. The difficulty which troubled her has not apparently disturbed D. W. Robertson, Jr., who has recently stated (A Preface to Chaucer, 463ff.) that "the dreamer and the knight are both aspects of the poet." Kemp Malone (Chapters on Chaucer) argues that "John of Gaunt's happy marriage with Blanche could not be represented as such but had to be turned into an extra-marital love affair for the sake of conformity to the conventions of courtly love," but this argument loses force if the love of the lady and the Black Knight was not consummated. Kittredge (Chaucer and His Poetry) refused to identify the dreamer with Chaucer. Samuel Schoebaum, "Chaucer's Black Knight," MLN, Vol. LXVIII (1953), 121-22, questions the whole occasional character of the poem.

leaving the rider suddenly on foot, walking away from the tree where he has apparently taken up his station, and never thinking of his mount again.

But Chaucer was after all a poet, and if he had any real learning in any field, it was in that of language and literature. His love of books has never been denied. According to the God of Love, there were sixty books in his own collection, and whether this be taken literally or not, it indicates a considerable collection, especially if we remember that one medieval manuscript might contain a number of works. I have already quoted the Eagle's accusation that after his day's work is done, Chaucer goes home and wears out his eyes over a book, leaving the world to wag on as it will. There is more than a hint of sympathy in his portrait of the studious, un-worldly Clerk, who

> was levere have at his beddes heed
> Twenty bookes, clad in blak or reed,
> Of Aristotle and his philosophie,
> Than robes riche, or fithele, or gay sautrie.

He also says,

> On bokes rede I ofte, as I yow tolde,[84]

and

> On bokes for to rede I me delyte,
> And to hem yive I feyth and ful credence,
> And in myn herte have hem in reverence,[85]

and when he was really interested he could say,

> To rede forth hit gan me so delite,
> That al that day me thoughte but a lyte.[86]

In the *Legend*, moreover, there is a rather remarkable passage in which books are honored as the depositories of accumulated race experience:

[84] "PF," l. 16.
[85] *LGW*, F, ll. 30–32.
[86] "PF," ll. 27–28.

> And yf that olde bokes were aweye,
> Yloren were of remembraunce the keye.[87]

But even literature furnished no guarantee of immortality, and the thought of mutability always haunted Chaucer.

> For hit ful depe is sonken in my mynde,
> With pitous hert in Englyssh to endyte
> This olde storie, in Latin which I fynde,
> Of quene Anelida and fals Arcite,
> That elde, which that al can frete and bite,
> As hit hath freten mony a noble storie,
> Hath nygh devoured out of our memorie.[88]

Even in foreign languages Chaucer's reading was not entirely what we would call "literary," for he must have been familiar with many of the Church Fathers mentioned by the Wife of Bath and others. From the fact that he has Januarie quote from it as he moves toward his legalized rape of May—

> "Rys up, my wyf, my love, my lady free!
> The turtles voys is herd, my dowve sweete;
> The wynter is goon with alle his reynes weete.
> Com forth now, with thyn eyen columbyn!
> How fairer been thy brestes than is wyn!"—

I should infer that he understood the true nature of the Song of Solomon, which is more than can be said for the seventeenth-century scholars who composed the pious allegorical chapter headings in the King James translation. And when he was proceeding to his "Tale of Melibee," he showed himself cognizant of the differences between the Four Gospels which still hold the attention of New Testament scholars today:

> "As thus: ye woot that every Evaungelist,
> That telleth us the peyne of Jhesu Crist,
> Ne seith nat alle thyng as his felawe dooth;
> But nathelees hir sentence is al sooth,

[87] F, ll. 25–26.   [88] "Anelida and Arcite," ll. 8–14.

And al acorden as in hire sentence,
Al be ther in hir tellyng difference.
For somme of hem seyn moore, and somme seyn lesse,
Whan they his pitous passioun expresse—
I meene of Mark, Mathew, Luc, and John—
But doubtlees hir sentence is al oon."

Chaucer was bilingual, for in his time French was both the language of the court—and the courts—and of the lower schools. He must have known it nearly as well as he knew English, and in view of the thoroughly French character of all his early models, it seems remarkable that he did not choose to write in it. Since he seems sometimes to have used a French "pony" in his Latin reading, his Latin was obviously not up to his French level, but he read widely in the language nevertheless—in Virgil and Ovid among others, but apparently not in Horace, whose spirit would seem closer to his than that of any other Latin writer. He telescopes Brutus and Cassius, but perhaps his most amusing blunder was made in "The House of Fame" when, mistaking the ablative plural *pernicibus*, from the adjective *pernix*, meaning "swift," for the ablative plural *perdicibus*, from the noun *perdix*, meaning partridge," he gave a goddess not swift wings but partridge wings! His Italian was certainly much better, yet he perpetrates a somewhat comparable "howler" when he mistakes a clean temple (*"Fu mondo il tempio"*) for one which smokes (*"Fumando il tempio"*). Greek he did not know (it would have been something of a miracle if, in his time, he had known it), as he himself virtually admits when, apologizing in advance for his fabliau tales, he writes in the General Prologue,

Eek Plato seith, whoso that kan hym rede,
The wordes moote be cosyn to the dede.

In "The Manciple's Tale" this is repeated almost word for word but without the admission:

The wise Plato seith, as ye may rede,
The word moot nede accorde with the dede.

Bernard F. Huppé has justly remarked[89] that when Plato said this, he was not thinking about what we call literary realism. "True words, according to Plato, will relate to the universal, the mathematical, and unchanging—they will be abstract." Very likely Chaucer did not know this; if he did, he chose to impose upon Plato an interpretation which, at the moment, was convenient to his own argument. In the same passage he declares that

> Crist spak hymself ful brode in hooly writ,
> And wel ye woot no vileynye is it.

He must certainly have known that there is nothing in the recorded utterances of Christ that could by any stretch of the imagination be called "broad," and that there is very little elsewhere in the New Testament to which that term could properly be applied, though there is a good deal in the Old. It may be, however, that Chaucer was speaking very loosely of Christ as if he were the author of the whole Bible: "In the beginning was the Word . . . ."

Chaucer's sympathies were too broad to be limited to the learned, or any other, class, and he does not seem wholly unsympathetic when he reports the sarcasm of the Miller toward the Clerks in "The Reeve's Tale":

> "Myn hous is streit, but ye han lerned art;
> Ye konne by argumentes make a place
> A myle brood of twenty foot of space."

Yet I do not think there is any doubt that books took first place among all his interests. I have already reported that he considers reading "better play" than chess or backgammon and that he prefers reading about human beings who have been turned into constellations to studying the stars at first hand. As Lounsbury remarked long ago, Chaucer rarely forfeits the interest and the sympathy of the modern reader except when he allows the preacher or the university lecturer to wrest the pen away from the artist. It may well be that his anxiety to acknowledge all his sources was not so much a matter of literary honesty (which would not have

[89] *A Reading of the Canterbury Tales* (State University of New York, 1964).

been involved, according to the usual standards of the time) as a desire to parade his learning. As Richard Strauss is said to have been beatifically tolerant of those who did not care for his music but hypersensitive to criticism of his handwriting, so Chaucer may well have been more proud of his knowledge than he was of his art. "What we call miracles and wonders of Art," so Longfellow has the Baron tell Paul Flemming in *Hyperion*, "are not so to him who created them, for they were created by the natural movement of his own great soul." And Bernard Shaw adds that "fine art, of any sort, is either easy or impossible." Obviously this is not true for everybody, and Stevenson testifies on the other side that easy writing makes hard reading. If anything in art can be called "natural" or divinely simple, Chaucer's great achievements would seem so. It is hard to believe that he ever did not know exactly what he was doing, and he so often found the inevitably right way of saying a thing that one finds it difficult to think of him as having sweat blood over his writing. Yet I fear one cannot be sure of this: he may even have been an indefatigable reviser whose art showed best in his completely successful way of covering his tracks. You can cite multitudinous sources even for the passages which seem to have been poured out most spontaneously—the bubbling self-revelations of the Wife, for example, and even the praise of spring at the beginning of the General Prologue.

Indeed, if reading had a serious competitor in Chaucer's affections, it must have been spring itself. If you had asked him which he loved more, I think he would have been troubled to know how to answer. In the *Legend* Prologue, however, he awards the palm to spring:

> ther is game noon
> That fro my bokes maketh me to goon,
> But yt be seldom on the holyday,
> Save, certeynly, whan that the month of May
> Is comen, and that I here the foules sprynge,
> Farwel my book, and my devocioun!

But many good students have felt like that.

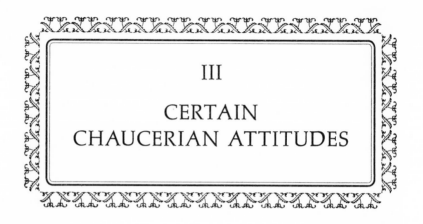

III

CERTAIN
CHAUCERIAN ATTITUDES

If Chaucer was a man of the court, what was his attitude toward courtly principles and ideals? I should say that so far as chivalry was concerned, he was fairly orthodox. It is not merely that in such stories as "The Knight's Tale" he presents a thoroughly chivalric view of life and love, nor that he preserves degree in his account of the Canterbury pilgrims,

> Me thynketh it acordaunt to resoun
> To telle yow al the condicioun
> Of ech of hem, so as they semed me,
> And whiche they weren, and of what degree.[1]

It is more significant, I think, that in "The Parliament of Fowls," after the three suitors have expressed the chivalric ideal of love, Chaucer should allow the goose and the cuckoo to utter unlovely common sense views and be roundly ridiculed for their pains. Only the turtle, who echoes the chivalric ideals of the noble birds,

[1] He preserves verisimiltude by having the pilgrims draw lots to determine who shall tell the first tale, but those were good medieval lots, who shared Chaucer's own respect for rank, and they knew better than to fall to anybody except the Knight, the man of highest rank in the company!

escapes ridicule. Troilus and Hector are typical knights, strong bold, young, and fresh, marked by

> "alle trouth and alle gentilesse,
> Wisdom, honour, fredom, and worthinesse."[2]

Valor and affability receive equal emphasis,[3] and in Hector's case there is a special emphasis upon virtue.[4] Chaucer had a fine chance to ridicule chivalry in his portrait of the Squire with his curled locks, wide-sleeved gown, and passionate devotion to his lady. It cannot be quite without significance that he passed it by.

He recoiled from the worst excesses of chivalry; he was a humorist, and he was a moderate man; he recoiled from excesses everywhere. Into the thoroughly conventional, though altogether charming, portrait of a lady in "The Book of the Duchess" he inserted a passage praising her for not sending her lovers on impossible missions to the Dry Sea and the Carrenare. But that would be a pretty flimsy basis upon which to construct an argument that he was anti-chivalric in general.

H. S. Bennett finds that

> He is content to allow a few members from the villages and townships to appear, but they are usually the aristocracy of the village—the miller, the reeve, or the carpenter. Similarly, the "solemn and grete fraternitee" of citizens receives meagre treatment, which is strange when we remember that Chaucer was born and bred in their midst, and that the part played by the great merchants and the great city-companies must have been constantly before his eyes.[5]

Nevertheless I think it possible to argue that Chaucer had some appreciation of the new forces that were stirring in his day, though I grant that without knowing medieval literature well, we are in danger of making this appreciation seem more radical and indi-

---

[2] *TC*, II, ll. 160–61; cf. also I, ll. 566–67; II, ll. 184–207; V, ll. 827–33.
[3] *TC*, II, ll. 184–207.
[4] *TC*, II, ll. 176–80.
[5] *Chaucer and the Fifteenth Century* (OUP, 1947); see also William Henry Schofield, *Chivalry in English Literature* (HUP, 1912).

vidual than it actually was. Chaucer's references to mobs are hardly more respectful than Shakespeare's, but it is not necessary to admire mobs in order to avoid being an aristocratic snob. In *The Canterbury Tales* the common people mingle with their betters in a pretty free-and-easy way, and the Knight and the Prioress accept the leadership of an innkeeper. Moreover, not even the Knight is more admired by Chaucer than the poor Parson and his "brother," the Plowman.

The tales bear out the promise of the Prologue, Notable is the Clerk's praise of Griselda, a poor girl raised to the highest position in the dukedom and specifically declared worthy of the honor. We are not permitted to hear the discussion among the pilgrims as to "which was the moste fre" (generous) in "The Franklin's Tale," but that the question should even be considered debatable with a knight, a squire, and a mere magic-working clerk as contenders surely means something, especially with the narrator himself declaring that

> Thus kan a squier doon a gentil dede
> As wel as kan a knyght, withouten drede.

And in "The Manciple's Tale" we are told uncompromisingly that a lady of high rank who is unchaste is no better than a common drab:

> Men leyn that oon as lowe as lith that oother.

When the Wife of Bath insists in her Prologue that true nobility depends not on blood but on behavior, she is not out of character—as a woman of the middle class she could hardly have believed anything else—but she does not stand alone. As Howard Patch points out,[6] the Parson denounces pride in riches and lineage in his tale ("Humble folk been Cristes freends"), and Chaucer himself says the same thing in "Gentilesse":

> Vyce may wel be heir to old richesse;
> But ther may no man, as men may wel see,

[6] *On Rereading Chaucer* (HUP, 1939), 189.

Bequethe his heir his vertuous noblesse
(That is appropred unto no degree
But to the first fader in magestee,
That maketh hem his heyres that him queme),
Al were he mytre, croune, or diademe.

Dante, Boccaccio, Jean de Meun, Wycliffe, Gower, and many others have been cited as supporting this point of view; Chaucer could not have denied it without flying in the face of the whole Christian thinking of his time on its highest level. The ideal gentleman was Jesus Christ.

Though Chaucer himself was called upon as late as 1390 to organize a tournament (he describes one in detail in "The Knight's Tale"), it has long been recognized that in his time chivalry was on its way out, being cherished more as a sentimental or nostalgic ideal than as something which anybody expected to have put into actual practice. But perhaps this had always been true of chivalry on its highest level; perhaps, alas, it is true of ideals in general. Though there has been no general agreement as to his possible "original," it has been recognized ever since 1907, when Manly published his famous article, "A Knight Ther Was,"[7] that Chaucer's Knight is a very special sort of Knight, devoting himself largely or wholly to religious wars, fought on the borders of the Christian world. In the old days it was often stated and believed that his tale, dealing as it does with young love, had no special applicability to the teller, being better suited to *a* knight than to our particular Knight, and even that Chaucer might better have assigned it to the Squire. Of late years, however, we have begun to see more depths in "The Knight's Tale" than we then saw,[8]

[7] *Transactions and Proceedings of the American Philological Association*, Vol. XXXVIII, 89–107, reprinted in Wagenknecht, *Chaucer: Modern Essays in Criticism*. See also Manly, *Some New Light*.

[8] See, for example, Charles Muscatine, "Form, Texture, and Meaning in Chaucer's 'Knight's Tale,'" *PMLA*, Vol. LXXV (1950), 911–29, reprinted in Wagenknecht, and, in a different form, in his *Chaucer and the French Tradition* (University of California Press, 1947); also R. M. Lumiansky, "Chaucer's Philosophical Knight," *Tulane Studies in English*, Vol. III (1952), 42–68. But Bernard Huppé's argument, in *A Reading of* The Canterbury Tales, that the Knight is displeased over his son's newfangled ways and tells a story "which has as its *sentence* not only

and I doubt that anybody would take up quite this position today.

In the General Prologue (and in what is surely the most masterly use not of a double but of a fourfold negative in all literature), Chaucer tells us of the Knight that

> He nevere yet no vileynye [discourtesy] ne sayde
> In al his lyf unto no maner wight.

It has sometimes been supposed that the Knight gives the lie to this when he interrupts "The Monk's Tale":

> "Hoo!" quod the Knyght, "good sire, namoore of this!
> That ye han seyd is right ynough, ywis,
> And muchel moore; for litel hevynesse
> Is right ynough to muche folk, I gesse.
> I seye for me, it is a great disese,
> Whereas men han been in greet welthe and ese,
> To heeren of hire sodeyn fal, allas!
> And the contrarie is joye and greet solas,
> As whan a man hath been in povre estaat,
> And clymbeth up and wexeth fortunat,
> And there abideth in prosperitee.
> Swich thyng is gladsom, as it thynketh me,
> And of swich thyng were goodly for to telle."

So accomplished a Chaucerian as Kemp Malone takes this as evidence "that our military hero has the taste of a child, or at any rate of a thoroughly unsophisticated person, when it comes to works of literary art. Tragedy he cannot abide." What the Knight wanted to read, in other words, was Alger books—*The Americanization of Edward Bok, The Autobiography of Andrew Carnegie.* This is a possible interpretation of the passage, but it is by no means the only one that can be made. I should not be willing to have my own appreciation of tragedy judged by my ability to relish the external and undeveloped "tragedies" rehearsed in "The Monk's Tale." Matthew Arnold did not have

---

a warning against the folly of young lovers but also instruction in the seriousness of life directed by Christian purposes" is not convincing.

"the taste of a child," but he objected to this type of tragedy—offering no true catharsis or relief in action—much as the Knight does. Since the Host is the only pilgrim who speaks up to support the Knight, we cannot be sure he speaks for all the company (the Host *is* an unsophisticated reader, though even he was deeply moved by the tragedy of "The Physician's Tale"), but with the prospect of a hundred narratives staring the whole company in the face, I should not be surprised to learn that if a poll could be taken, we should find the Knight's position pretty generally supported. He was the only man in the company who had sufficient standing to "stint" the Monk (we are to understand, I believe, that Chaucer, whom the Host himself "stinted" in his tale of "Sir Thopas," was considerably less formidable, but I shall return to this incident later), and the provocation was great. The only other occasion on which the Knight intervenes is to make peace between the Host and the Pardoner after the quarrel which follows "The Pardoner's Tale," and even if we do not accept Kittredge's interpretation of the Pardoner's condition at this point,[9] there can be no question that here the Knight does exemplify "curtesie" to an outstanding degree. If Principal Adeney of Manchester was right when he found mercy to the utterly undeserving the most touching form of Grace, then the Knight's christianism in this act can hardly be unquestioned.

It has also been argued that because of the specialized career he assigned to his Knight, Chaucer must, like Wycliffe, have disapproved of all wars except religious wars.[10] (Legouis once remarked[11] that there was "not a single patriotic line" in Chaucer's work and no disparaging reference to any foreigner as such.) The exemption from condemnation of religious wars would not help Chaucer much with twentieth-century readers, who are likely to find such conflicts the most indefensible of all, though unfor-

[9] "Chaucer's Pardoner," *Atlantic Monthly*, Vol. LXXII (1893), 829–33, reprinted in Wagenknecht.

[10] See Roger S. Loomis, "Was Chaucer a Laodicean?" in *Essays and Studies in Honor of Carleton Brown* (New York University Press, 1940), reprinted in Shoeck and Taylor, *Chaucer Criticism: Canterbury Tales*.

[11] In *Geoffrey Chaucer* (Dutton, 1913).

tunately many of them still seem able to embrace war with alacrity
when it is theoretically waged in support of or in opposition to
some such modern secular faith as "communism" or "democracy."
But though Chaucer says nothing about the Knight's possible
service in the Hundred Years War, we cannot be sure that the line

> Ful worthy was he in his lordes werre

was not meant to imply that he participated, and the Squire certainly did, without any expression of disapproval on his creator's
part.[12]

Many years ago Lounsbury wrote that Chaucer "was a soldier,
and his sympathies lay naturally with the military order. Many
of the tenets of Wycliffe found favor with the class with which
he had become affiliated. There is no reason to suppose that in
this matter he differed from his brothers in arms." On this ground,
Lounsbury even believed that Chaucer "would naturally take and
present the most unfavorable view of the clerical body, and a
correspondingly favorable one of the military." Much more recently, Florence R. Scott has suggested[13] that since Chaucer was
the son of a vintner, "his sympathies must originally have been
with the 'victuallers,'" who were always the peace party. "However, his marriage, probably in 1366, to Philippa Roet . . . must
have largely neutralized the interest, since to Gaunt was attached
the strong group of 'anti victuallers,' the party always interested

[12] Gardiner Stillwell and Henry J. Webb, "Chaucer's Knight and the Hundred
Years War," *MLN*, Vol. LIX (1944), 45–57, are convincing, on the whole, in
their reply to Loomis, though their assumption that the Knight *must* have served
in the Hundred Years War because the Squire did will not hold. Surely they
cannot intend us to believe that the Squire attended his father in *all* his campaigns.
A later article by Webb, "A Reinterpretation of Chaucer's Theseus," *RES*, Vol.
XXXIII (1947), 289–96, which argues that Chaucer intended us to think of the
Theseus of "The Knight's Tale" as a cruel tyrant and remember his later relations
with Ariadne, does not make its point. D. W. Robertson, Jr., goes to the other
extreme when (*A Preface to Chaucer*, 284–85) he classifies Theseus with Constance, Griselda, and St. Cecilia as "distinguished by virtue rather than by heroic
action." He admits that Theseus is a mighty conqueror but finds that "his physical
heroism is passed over lightly and his wisdom and mercy are stressed instead." This
is true as far as it goes, but the nature of the story being what it is, what else could
Chaucer have done?

[13] "Chaucer and the Parliament of 1386," *Speculum*, Vol. XVIII (1943),
80–86.

in foreign wars," and she thinks that this conflict may, in later years, have caused Chaucer considerable mental anguish.

This is as it may be, but I doubt that any Chaucer scholar today would quite endorse Lounsbury's judgment. It is true that Chaucer lived in rude times, and that rude times develop strong stomachs in those whom they do not destroy. His own father was kidnapped in youth, and he himself was beaten and robbed more than once toward the end of his life. During the riots of 1381 he lived close to pillaging and burning, and even when things were running smoothly, he may have seen violence in the streets. It is true, too, that, like the Squire, he participated in the Hundred Years War, and was captured and ransomed by the King at a cost less than what was paid for a good war horse, which indicates that he was a gentleman but young and unimportant. Yet he did not go on to knighthood, nor does war seem to have inspired his muse.

"He was a poet of love," writes Percy Van Dyke Shelly, "not of adventure or of conquest."[14] The classification is traditional and basically sound, but though war is of all forces the one most opposed to love (and most friendly to lust), in literature the antithesis is not, unfortunately, clear-cut. Though Chaucer does not describe them, numerous passages make the point that Troilus was inspired to mighty feats of arms by his love for Criseyde, and even the Squire,

> In Flaundres, in Artoys, and Pycardie,

had

> born hym weel, as of so litel space,
> In hope to stonden in his lady grace.

If J. Leslie Hotson's interpretation of "The Tale of Melibee"[15] is accepted, Chaucer produced that piece as a pacifist tract to deter John of Gaunt from embarking upon an invasion of Castille.

[14] *The Living Chaucer* (University of Pennsylvania Press, 1940).
[15] "The Tale of Melibeus and John of Gaunt," *SP*, Vol. XVIII (1918), 429–52. For another interpretation, see Gardiner Stillwell, "The Political Meaning of Chaucer's 'Tale of Melibee,'" *Speculum*, Vol. XIX (1944), 433–44.

This is highly speculative and has not been generally accepted, but whether it was occasioned or not, "Melibee" is clearly a pacifist work, and we cannot prove that Chaucer did not sympathize with the views expressed in it by simply pointing out that it is, after all, a translation. If he did not sympathize with it, why did he undertake the not inconsiderable labor of translating it (in the place of some militaristic work which he could easily have found) and making it a part of *The Canterbury Tales?* I am of course not arguing that Chaucer was a pacifist in the sense in which his friend John Gower was a pacifist, but this seems to me less significant than I should perhaps otherwise consider it because Chaucer, like Shakespeare, was, I am sure, the kind of man unlikely to stake out a "strong" position on any point. It is difficult, however, to think of him as a quarreler. In any specific situation I am sure he would be an influence for conciliation, not exacerbation. And if his idealization of the Knight seems out of line with this, I can only reply that it is not unparalleled. John Greenleaf Whittier *was* a pacifist, ideationally speaking, but he extravagantly admired General Gordon and, to a lesser degree, even the General Sherman who ravaged Georgia from Atlanta to the sea.

How much is known or can be inferred about Chaucer's political views or attitude toward public affairs in general? As a civil servant and a member of the court circle, he was certainly in a favorable position to form views, though expressing them might have been something else again. He grew up in an age of English glory under Edward III, and he spent his last years, under Richard II, amid conditions which caused many men to despair. Nor was it England alone on which the sun seemed to be setting; things were bad on the Continent too. Says Professor Loomis:

He was in daily contact with men on opposite sides of the bitter struggle for power between King Richard and his uncles, and yet, as Professor Hulbert has brought out, he seems to have kept the friendship of both parties. Kuhl has suggested that Chaucer's selection of the five guildsmen in the General Prologue was dictated by the consideration that these guilds were neutral in the conflict between the victuallers and the nonvictuallers, and so gave no offense to either party. To retain, as Chaucer did, his pensions and perquisites during the last years of Richard's reign and to have them immediately confirmed by Richard's foe and conqueror implies a prudent neutrality and superlative tact.

It has been conjectured that it was because the Duke of Gloucester had temporarily come into power that Chaucer lost his position in the customs, but this is by no means certain. He himself was a member of the stormy Parliament of 1386, which slaughtered Thomas Usk and his own former colleague in the customs, Sir Nicholas Brembre.[16] Loomis finds it "little short of amazing that writing the General Prologue within six years of the Peasants' Revolt, this poet of the court should sketch for us a representative peasant, the Plowman, not as a loafer, a scamp, a bolshevik, a sower of class hatred, but as a model of all the social and Christian virtues." Perhaps. But may it not also have been that Chaucer and the court party were thus proclaiming what peasants "ought" to be, as the faithful Negroes who "keep their place" were lauded in *The Birth of a Nation?*

Some topical references have been generally accepted in Chaucer—"the murmure and the cherles rebellyng" and "Jack Straw and his meynee."[17] When the poet attached his wicked Pardoner to the convent at Rouncival, he must certainly have known that that establishment was in bad odor. There are other possible topical references of a noncontroversial nature, such as

> . . . the tempest at hir hoom-comynge

and

> Right as our firste lettre is now an A,[18]

[16] John P. McCall and George Rudisill, Jr., "The Parliament of 1386 and Chaucer's Trojan Parliament," *JEGP,* Vol. LVIII (1959), 276–88, try to show Chaucer, "astounded by the vindictiveness of his friends' political adversaries," giving an oblique, hostile picture of the English parliament as the Trojan parliament.
[17] *CT,* I, l. 2459; VII, l. 3394.
[18] *CT,* I, l. 884; *TC,* I, l. 172.

which may well refer to Queen Anne, and perhaps, though less certainly, a reference to the Black Death in the Reeve's portrait:

They were adrad of hym as of the deeth.

There cannot be much doubt that "Lak of Stedfastnesse" reflects Chaucer's unhappiness concerning the personal misgovernment of Richard II, nor that the balade "Truth" gives about the only advice any sensible man could give under the conditions which prevailed when it was written, and though "The Former Age" is too conventional to stand alone, the sentiments expressed in it seem quite in harmony with those in the other pieces. There are more controversial matters too, such as Hotson's interpretation of "The Nun's Priest's Tale" as containing an allegory of the Gloucester murder, and Manly's and Lilian Winstanley's views of "Sir Thopas" as having been directed against the Flemings, and most interpretations of "The Parliament of Fowls" assume considerable interest in public affairs on Chaucer's part.[19]

Any or all of these interpretations may be rejected, but if we do reject them, I think we must at the same time allow that there may still be many unrecognized references to fourteenth-century matters in Chaucer's various writings which his contemporaries understood but which the passing of time has veiled from our eyes. I do not mean by this that he was what we call a "topical" writer. I am sure that he was not. If he thought about the matter in such terms at all (which I doubt), I think he was more concerned to be in tune with humanity and with the universe than he was to be in tune with the passing hour. But the mere fact that he does not seem to have been notably more prone to refer to topical interests of a noncontroversial nature than to those which might conceivably have landed him in hot water

---

[19] J. Leslie Hotson, "Colfox vs. Chauntecleer," *PMLA*, Vol. XXXIX (1924), 762–81, reprinted in Wagenknecht; J. M. Manly, " 'Sir Thopas': A Satire," *Essays and Studies by Members of the English Association*, Vol. XIII (OUP, 1928); Lilian Winstanley, ed., "*The Prioress's Tale*" and "*Sir Thopas*" (Cambridge University Press, 1922). Charles O. MacDonald, "An Interpretation of Chaucer's 'Parlement of Foules,' " *Speculum*, Vol. XXX (1955), 444–57, reprinted in Wagenknecht, includes a summary of the views put forth up to this time.

should give us pause when we are tempted to regard him as overcautious.[20]

Chaucer's attitude toward social life would seem to have been at best one of tolerance. I am sure he did not always look upon the ground as if he were searching for a hare, but the consistency with which he slides over descriptions of feasts and social assemblies cannot be entirely without signficance. I know that he uses the rhetorical device of *occupatio,* or refusal to narrate, in other connections also, but the frequency with which he employs it in this connection is still suggestive.

> Me list nat of the chaf, ne of the stree,
> Maken so long a tale as of the corn.
> What sholde I tellen of the roialtee
> At mariage, or which cours goth biforn;
> Who bloweth in a trumpe or in an horn?
> The fruyt of every tale is for to seye:
> They ete, and drynke, and daunce, and synge, and pleye.[21]

He is very sarcastic about the social ambitions of the Tradesmen's wives in the General Prologue. In "The Shipman's Tale" there is a frank (and very masculine) pronouncement that the ambitions of the merchant's wife

> is a thyng that causeth more dispence
> Than worth is al the chiere and reverence
> That men hem doon at festes and at daunces.

[20] Sidney Hayes Cox, "Chaucer's Cheerful Cynicism," *MLN,* Vol. XXXVI (1921), 475–81, is a cheap and gamin-like article, whose only significance now is its demonstration that not even the learned journals were wholly immune to the spirit of the Jazz Age. Margaret Schlauch, "Chaucer's Doctrine of Kings and Tyrants," *Speculum,* Vol. XX (1945), 133–56, examines the political theory and practice of Chaucer's time in an attempt to determine his attitude. "Faithful he no doubt was to the king he served, but he could scarcely have been ignorant of the dangers implicit in the theory of absolute kingship which Richard was developing." Professor Schlauch tends to find "Lak of Stedfastnesse," LGW, G, ll. 353–76, and other passages in line with Wycliffe's ideas "that righteousness or a state of grace is the one true basis of lordship" and that the functions of a king are "to keep order in the state, to subdue rebels by force, to reward those who do justice, to keep peace within and without the realm."

[21] CT, II, ll. 701–707 ("The Man of Law's Tale"). See also I, ll. 2197–2208 ("The Knight's Tale"); V, ll. 59–75 ("The Squire's Tale").

Swiche salutaciouns and countenances
Passen as dooth a shadwe upon the wal.

And since this tale was originally intended to be told by the Wife
of Bath,[22] I think we may be sure that though the voice may
be Jacob's voice, the hands are the hands of Esau. With these passages may be placed the account of the gossips who come to comfort Criseyde in her tribulation,

Right as a man is esed for to feele,
For ache of hed, to clawen hym on his heele![23]

Yet Chaucer does not seem in any sense unfriendly to the Franklin, who was a true son of Epicurus, and in whose house it snowed
meat and drink. (There is no indication that we are supposed to
think of him as either a drunkard or a glutton.) I would gather,
however, that though Chaucer had no difficulty with social contacts, he was not unhappy when left alone, and that, like most
thoughtful men, he found informal conversation with some individual human being who chanced to interest him more rewarding
than the stilted hypocrisies of formal social intercourse on a
large scale.

Chaucer gives the impression of having placed a very modest
estimation upon his own achievements, and in a sense I think he
did, but, as I hope to show, his self-depreciation can be decep-
tive. In "The House of Fame" he pokes fun at himself through
the Eagle (who, generally speaking, is made to treat him as if he
were feeble-minded): his verse is light and common and sometimes syllabically imperfect. In the *Legend* he is only gleaning
(perhaps calling up his memories of the Book of Ruth) what
those who preceded him have forgotten, and on one occasion
at least even the little wit he has is described as having gone to
sleep. In *Troilus and Criseyde*[24] he is only following his "auctor"
—that mysterious "Lollius" who has furnished so much material

22 "He moot us clothe, and he moote us arraye" (the "he" referring to a husband) has meaning only in the mouth of a married woman, and the Wife of Bath
is the only woman in the company who has ever been married.
23 *TC*, IV, ll. 727–28.   24 II, ll. 15–18.

to scholars who must otherwise have remained unemployed—and disclaims both praise and blame. And in *The Canterbury Tales* we are told, among other things, that he has little wit and little skill in metre or rime.[25] When he comes to a crisis he nearly always apologizes: he has no English suitable to describe the malice of Donegild; he is unable to picture the beauty of Canacee; he cannot "ryme in Englyssh proprely" the sorrows of Palamon; and he will not even attempt to describe the knight on the brass stede in "The Squire's Tale."

He seems greatly to have feared the danger of boring his reader.

> But now, paraunter, som man wayten wolde
> That every word, or soonde, or look, or cheere
> Of Troilus that I rehercen sholde,
> In al this while unto his lady deere.
> I trowe it were a long thyng for to here;
> Or of what wight that stant in swich disjoynte,
> His wordes alle, or every look, to poynte.[26]

It is possible to explain the frequent use of *occupatio* in the *Legend* on the ground that here Chaucer was not greatly interested in his subject, but surely no such explanation would serve for "The Knight's Tale," where I have noted eight examples. In "The Squire's Tale," which so captivated two of his greatest successors among English poets—Spenser and Milton—he makes a special point of not holding back the kernel of the story until after the reader has been worn out.

> The knotte why that every tale is toold,
> If it be taried til that lust be coold
> Of hem that han it after herkned yoore,
> The savour passeth ever lenger the moore,
> For fulsomenesse of his prolixitee;
> And by the same resoun, thynketh me,
> I sholde to the knotte condescende,
> And maken of his waylkyng soone an ende.

---

[25] II, ll. 33ff.   [26] *TC*, III, ll. 491-97.

I am sure that, for all his love of books, Chaucer was an impatient reader as well as writer, and that he skipped freely when his attention wandered. In "The Legend of Hypsipyle and Medea" he writes of Jason:

> But whoso axeth who is with hym gon,
> Lat hym go read Argonautycon.

And at one point in *Troilus and Criseyde* he makes the prophetic Cassandra talk just as he does:

> "But how this Meleagre gan to dye
> Through his moder, wol I yow naught telle,
> For al to longe it were for to dwelle."[27]

On the other hand, Chaucer has an author's honest pride in his work: he knows what he is about, and he knows that he knows it. When, in the House of Fame, he is asked whether he has come in search of renown, there is more than a trace of self-sufficiency in his answer:

> "I cam noght hyder, graunt mercy,
> For no such cause, by my hed!
> Sufficeth me, as I were ded,
> That no wight have my name in honde.
> I wot myself best how y stonde;
> For what I drye, or what I thynke,
> I wol myselven al hyt drynke,
> Certeyn, for the more part,
> As fer forth as I kan myn art."

In the *Troilus* he twice explains what he fears may be taken for doubtful procedure, and in closing he expresses the author's hope that as time goes on his poem will not be miswritten or rendered unintelligible.[28] All this is quite in harmony with the humorous curse pronounced upon a careless scribe in "Chaucers Wordes unto Adam, His Owne Scriveyn." In this light, I think that while

---

[27] V, ll. 1483–84.
[28] II, ll. 22–28, 666–79; V, ll. 1793–99.

we may take the self-sufficiency of the "Fame" passage I have just quoted at face value, we may discount the statement that Chaucer would be well pleased to have his name forgotten after his death. It must not be forgotten that when he said this, he had just witnessed the high-handed and arbitrary treatment which Fame metes out to her petitioners; if *this* be renown, what sensible man could care to touch it?

In *The Canterbury Tales* Chaucer assigns to himself as narrator, first, the "drasty" and "lewed" tale of "Sir Thopas," which the Host could not bear to hear through (the Monk is the only other narrator whose tale is uninterrupted, and surely if one must be censured, one would rather submit to a "verray, parfit gentil knyght" than to a rude, uncultured innkeeper), and, second, "The Tale of Melibee," which the moral and intellectual leaders of American youth in our colleges generally pass over in favor of "The Miller's Tale" and which many Ph.D.'s in English do not even pretend ever to have read through. Once upon a time it was the fashion in some quarters to regard "Melibee" as Chaucer's way of laughing last at the Host; if he would not be bored by the lighthearted "Sir Thopas," then he must submit to be bored instead by the far more inimical "Melibee." This is patently wrong from almost any conceivable point of view. To begin with, the Host did *not* have to listen to "Melibee"; since he had interrupted Chaucer once, there was surely no reason why he might not have interrupted him twice, and, in the second place, there is no reason whatever to suppose that either he or the other pilgrims found anything wrong with it; in fact, the Host specifically expresses his interest in it, though he bases his appreciation upon quite nonliterary grounds. It represents a type of literature which the Middle Ages in general admired, and anyone who believes that Chaucer did not will be obliged to explain not only why he wrote "Melibee" but also why he wrote "The Parson's Tale," which appeals to the same kind of taste and was not "occasioned" by anything that happened on the pilgrimage, and why he translated Boethius. As for the "Melibee" being a joke on the Host, I suppose it is barely conceivable that a James Joyce might have been capable of spinning out a joke to such dismal length, but the impatient Chaucer would surely know that if he were to attempt such a thing, the joke would be on him. I express no opinion concerning the difference in taste between the fourteenth century and the twentieth on such matters, merely contenting myself by recalling Chesterton's useful reminder that the age in which we live *is* an age and not the Day of Judgment.

I said a moment ago that if one were to be interrupted in telling one's tale, one would prefer to be interrupted by the Knight rather than by the Host, and under ordinary circumstances this would be true but not under those which Chaucer has created. For the Knight's views would need to be seriously regarded, whereas the Host, a man of splendid practical facility who regards himself as a well-nigh universal authority, cannot be taken seriously as a literary critic, as his numerous malapropisms show.[29] To Chaucer and his sophisticated readers, in other words, it is actually a compliment that the Host should not be able to endure "Sir Thopas."

For this "drasty" rime is a burlesque on metrical romances, which were an essentially aristocratic type of literature. If the Host was familiar with them at all, he probably knew them in shortened, popularized versions intended for middle-class readers; *a priori* one would expect him to be more at home with fabliaux. But suppose he did enjoy the romances as he knew them; the more he liked them the more he would resent a burlesque. If he did not know them, "Sir Thopas" would be meaningless to him, and if he did, he would be likely to regard it as a species of literary blasphemy, just as unlearned persons whose lives display no evidence of concern with religion are often sincerely shocked by a humorous treatment of sacred themes which a more sophisticated but also far more devout person might thoroughly enjoy. And incidentally nobody was more capable of employing sacred subjects for humorous purposes when occasion arose, and quite

---

[29] Chaucer slips, I think, in his characterization, when, in *CT*, IV, ll. 15–20, he allows the Host a knowledge of formal rhetorical terms. The point of view expressed here is in character but the language employed is not.

without the slightest suggestion of fundamental irreverence, than the same Geoffrey Chaucer with whom we are here concerned.[30]

Look at the Host's approach to the Lady Prioress when he asks her to tell her tale:

> "My lady Prioresse, by your leve,
> So that I wiste I sholde yow nat greve,
> I wolde demen that ye tellen sholde
> A tale next, if so were that ye wolde.
> Now wol ye vouche sauf, my lady deere?"

Robinson rightly calls this the politest speech in English literature. But it makes politeness more odious than rudeness because it is so absurdly overdone. I used to think that the joke was on the Prioress, and that the Host, who saw through her imitation of the manners of the court, was making fun of her. But this is not the case. He takes the counterfeit at face value, and he is tremendously impressed. He is not quite sure that a religious is a human being anyway, and when he is obliged to address her, he goes at it with all the gaucherie of a newly-made father who handles the baby as if he supposed her to be made of china and liable to break. How sharp is the contrast between his absurd vocal genuflections and the dignified response of the Prioress:

> "Gladly," quod she, and seyde as ye shul heere.

Few poets have ever made a single word accomplish more.

Possibly the puzzling aspects of the Introduction to "The Man of Law's Tale" might be explained in the same way. The passage[31] is too long to quote in its entirety, but its essence is as follows.

---

[30] George Williams, *A New View of Chaucer* (Duke University Press, 1965), Chapter VIII, explains Harry Bailly's anger and his use of such words as "drasty" and "lewed" on the ground that his sense of propriety has been outraged by what he considers the homosexual characteristics of Sir Thopas. He is not the first critic to see perversion in this character (cf. Robinson's note, pp. 736–37, with the references listed), though certainly nobody else has carried the interpretation to such lengths nor supposed that Sir Thopas was intended to represent Richard II. But even if he is right, and even if Manly and Miss Winstanley, either or both, are right in seeing satire on the Flemings, "Sir Thopas" is still a burlesque on the romances.

[31] *CT*, II, ll. 39–98.

Called upon by the Host to fulfill the contract to which, like all the pilgrims, he had subscribed in the General Prologue, the Man of Law is almost servile in proclaiming his willingness to comply, but finds it difficult to dredge up a "thrifty" tale because

> "Chaucer, thogh he can but lewedly
> On metres and on ryming craftily,
> Hath seyd hem in swich Englissh as he kan
> Of olde tyme, as knoweth many a man;
> And if he have noght seyd hem, leve brother,
> In o book, he hath seyd hem in another."

Hereupon follows a list of Chaucer's writings, after which the speaker makes the special point that there is one kind of story that Chaucer does not tell, that which deals with twisted sex relationships like the tales of Canacee and "Tyro Appollonius."[32]

> "And therefore he, of ful avysement,
> Nolde nevere write in none of his sermons
> Of swiche unkynde abhomynacions,
> Ne I wol noon reherce, if that I may."

Finally, the Man of Law declares,

> "I speke in prose, and lat him rymes make,"

whereupon he proceeds to recite a saint's legend, which is in rime royal, and whose connection with either his profession or his character as suggested in the General Prologue is far from clear.

We must pass over for the moment the question why Chaucer here chooses to surround himself with an aura of purity and the suggestion that he may have been hitting at Gower, who had told stories concerning these characters in his *Confessio Amantis*, and who, about this time, removed from the manuscript of that work a passage containing a compliment to Chaucer. Our present concern is with the Man of Law's superior attitude toward Chaucer as

---

[32] Chaucer did start to tell a story about Canacee in "The Squire's Tale" but broke it off before coming to the point at which incest might have entered it. Did he leave it unfinished because of the stand he had taken (for whatever reason) in the passage under consideration?

a mediocre poet who apparently strove to make up in bulk what he lacked in quality.

A number of years ago, Dr. William L. Sullivan, then a graduate student in one of my Chaucer classes, grappled with this problem and came up with conclusions which became an article in one of the learned journals.[33] Mr. Sullivan did not read even the reference to tales of incest as a compliment to Chaucer on the speaker's part, placing it instead in the "one-thing-I-can-say-for-him" class. It may be a compliment to a writer to call him wholesome, and it may be a compliment to call him prolific, but if that is all that can be said in his favor, it is a little like praising a girl's appearance because she has pretty hair. Accepting Manly's tentative identification of the Man of Law with Thomas Pynchbeck, Mr. Sullivan saw Chaucer as undertaking to ridicule one who set up pretensions as a literary critic without possessing either the taste or the knowledge required to back them up. The criticism of Chaucer redounds, therefore, to his credit, for it is that of an ignorant impostor whose superficial knowledge the reader is supposed to laugh at. On this basis Mr. Sullivan even attempted to explain the lack of complete correspondence between what the Man of Law says Chaucer wrote and what we know him to have written from other sources. It is, he says, as if an ignorant pretender to knowledge of twentieth-century literature should carelessly speak of *Murder in the Cathedral* as *Death Comes for the Archbishop*.

Not all readers will accept this interpretation. E. C. Knowlton, for example,[34] was much impressed by the Man of Law. But the same class in which Mr. Sullivan was enrolled had a student named Patricia Hughes, who came up with a commentary on Knowlton's article which, to my way of thinking, deserved publication as much as Mr. Sullivan's did, though, so far as I know, she never attempted to secure it. Mrs. Hughes saw the Man of Law as a pompous, conceited man who looked upon himself as Chaucer's intellectual superior. If they knew and disliked each other before the pilgrim-

[33] "Chaucer's Man of Law as a Literary Critic," *MLN*, Vol. LXVIII (1953), 1–8.

[34] "Chaucer's Man of Law," *JEGP*, Vol. XXIII (1924), 83–93.

age began (Pynchbeck again), then he might well delight in seizing an opportunity to show that he could beat Chaucer at his own game. So, having disparaged the professional, and even complimented him in an underhanded way, he attempts to put him off his guard by disparaging his own abilities too: "I speke in prose." After that introduction nobody will expect much of him, and he can carry the war into the enemy's country by relating a romance quite as Chaucer himself might have done it, thus out-Chaucering Chaucer at his own game.

Here, it will be observed, is a new interpretation of "I speke in prose." If Mrs. Hughes's view be accepted, not only is the problem of the old contradiction resolved, but an intensely dramatic situation has been developed. Moreover, the story has itself become a dramatic utterance, and the question why Chaucer assigned such an unsuitable subject to the Man of Law need no longer be considered. But however all this may be, it must be clear that when Chaucer makes fun of himself, he deals only in allegations which, as he must well have known, no intelligent reader could possibly credit. If he had actually been "lewed," he surely would not have allowed the Eagle to call him that. As Kemp Malone says, "Chaucer's audience knew perfectly well that he was a man of learning and anything but a lazy-bones." It is only those who know both their capacities and their limitations better than their critics can possibly be expected to know them who can accept themselves with sufficient completeness to be able to smile at criticism.

I must say again that none of this means that I think Chaucer was an arrogant man. Indeed the arrogant man has not accepted himself; in his own eyes, he is perpetually on trial, and he throws his weight about as a means of avoiding coming face to face with himself. I am sure that some of Chaucer's humility in *The Canterbury Tales* and elsewhere is perfectly straightforward, and I agree with Donald R. Howard that he was "a bourgeois addressing his social betters."

Chaucer was a bourgeois who successfully established himself as a civil servant, and . . . he was a poet who wrote for the court.

His aristocratic audience, which certainly admired him, would still have looked upon him as a social inferior.

Doubtless he looked upon himself as their social inferior also, but unless he was a complete fool (which he certainly was not), he must also have known that his special gift had placed him sufficiently above them in the aristocracy which is reserved for genius alone so that such things did not need to trouble him any more— and indeed much less—than he was troubled by the very different and far more profound and spiritually healthy humility that he felt toward God. Nothing has been said about Chaucer in this aspect that is more penetrating or knowledgeable than one of Sister M. Madeleva's comments on the "Astrolabe":

> The lad is not to rate him too highly, is not to think him more learned than he is. He is to understand clearly that his father neither discovered nor developed any of the scientific principles that he is giving him in simple form. . . . "I n'am but a lewd compilator of the labour of olde astrologiens, and have it translated in myn Englissh oonly for thy doctrine. And with this swerd shall I sleen envie." The sentence leaps out of the text with sudden, fierce vindictiveness, quells malice with a gesture and falls laughing back into the context, a shining blade of truth beside its happy sheath of humor. Nothing could be more typically Chaucerian.

What I am saying, of course, is that I believe Chaucer was sufficiently confident of his powers so that he did not need to go about testing them, though when a great occasion arose, he was nearly always able to rise with it. We can hardly remind ourselves too often that he was not what we call a professional writer and that therefore he did not need to concern himself with "the book industry" or "the literary market place." Neither did he worry about reviewers, and, above all else, he certainly did not think of himself as "the Father of English Poetry" or "the Well of English Undefiled." Some of these advantages, like some aspects of his temperament, he shared with Shakespeare, but he was still more fortunate, for Shakespeare did need to write when his theater required a new play, while, except for a possible occasional special commission like *The Legend of Good Women*, Chaucer wrote only when the spirit moved him. And, for that matter, he never finished *The Legend of Good Women*.

We do not know how far he ever formulated his literary theory.[35] He obviously had a certain temperamental bent toward realism and simplicity.

"Thyng that I speke, it moot be bare and pleyn."[36]

He was a master of plain style and of the casual and straightforward, even when it had to be achieved by the use of very artful devices. His development was away from formalism, not toward it, and in no sense was he, like Spenser, a "poet's poet." It was not that the rhetorical "high style" of the rhetoricians under whom he served his apprenticeship was ever beyond him,[37] but as he grew older he used it less and less, as when he invokes Gaufred de Vinsauf in "The Nun's Priest's Tale" and describes the fall of a cock in terms grandiloquent enough to serve for the fall of Troy, or uses rhetorical methods of indicating the passing of time but laughs at them as he uses them, as in

> The dayes honour, and the hevenes yë,
> The nyghtes foo—al this clepe I the sonne—

or

> But sodeynly bigonne revel newe
> Til that the brighte sonne loste his hewe;

[35] The most ambitious attempt to do it for him is that of Alan Renoir, "Tradition and Moral Realism: Chaucer's Conception of the Poet," *Neophilologica*, Vol. XXXV (1963), 199–210. See also Whitney Hastings Wells, "Chaucer as a Literary Critic," *MLN*, Vol. XXXIX (1924), 255–68.

[36] *CT*, V, l. 720.

[37] Malone, *Chapters on Chaucer*, 244–46, comments illuminatingly on Chaucer's transition from high style to plain style within the very first metrical paragraph of the General Prologue. For further comment on Chaucer's preference for colloquialism, see Charles Muscatine in Brewer's *Chaucer and Chaucerians* and the two articles cited there: Margaret Schlauch, "Chaucer's Colloquial English: Its Structural Traits," *PMLA*, Vol. LXVI (1952), 1103–16, and Dorothy Everett, "Chaucer's 'Good Ear,'" *Essays in Mediaeval Literature* (OUP, 1955).

For th'orisonte hath reft the sonne his lyght,—
This is as muche to seye as it was nyght![38]

(Kittredge noted, as evidence of Chaucer's "artistic economy,"
that all Dryden's paraphrases are longer than the original.) Sometimes he apologizes for disregarding the rules but one senses no
true penitence in him, and one often feels that he deliberately tries
for a certain amount of irregularity or imperfection. Even when
his materials are highly romantic, unexpected touches of realism
will break in. Cook long ago pointed out some of these in the
descriptions of Ligurge and Emetreus in "The Knight's Tale,"[39]
and if Kittredge was right about the wicker house in "The House
of Fame" being Irish in origin, then Chaucer was capable of drawing even fairy tale materials from his own observation.

"Faerye" was not a closed realm to him, as "The Squire's Tale"
and "The Wife of Bath's Tale" show, but it was a homely kind of
"faerye" which held him, more German than French. Though he
was a medieval man, he would never have recognized the medieval
dream world of *Pelléas and Mélisande*; he would have felt much
more at home with *Kristin Lavransdatter* and *The Master of Hest-
viken*. Neither could he have cared much for the kind of French
poetry that Debussy, Fauré, Duparc, and other Romantic French
composers loved to set. I have said that he commanded "high
style" whenever he chose to do so—Brewer finds him in perfect
command of it at the beginning of each book of "The Knight's
Tale"—but what Poe understood by poetry lay quite outside his
range; he could never have written "Annabel Lee," and it is no
accident that Poe had nothing of consequence to say about him.
Nevil Coghill rightly remarks that

imagery as we know it in Shakespeare, Donne, Milton, or
Keats, the imagery of broken opalescences, half-tones, impre-
cise suggestion, sudden wonder, extended learning, remote
allusion and, above all, the imagery of metaphor that shows

[38] *TC*, II, ll. 904–905; *CT*, V, ll. 1015–18 ("The Friar's Tale").
[39] See Robinson's note on *CT*, I, ll. 2095ff. on p. 678 of his edition.

one thing instantly in terms of another with a flash of revelation

was not for Chaucer.[40]

Machaut, Froissart, Deschamps, and *The Romance of the Rose* ruled Chaucer's art in his first phase, and Gaufred de Vinsauf and Matthieu de Vendôme were the rhetoricians who reduced their practices to dogma.[41] Since they were concerned wholly with means and effects and have nothing to say about content or meaning, it is possible to deplore their influence and to wonder whether Chaucer might have risen higher, or developed more rapidly, if he had not known them, or if the influential poets of his early years had been of a different and higher type. About all we can be sure of is that the poets did furnish him with models and the rhetoricians suggest a way of using them; whether another set of either or both might have served better, we cannot, in the absence of verifiable evidence, be sure. Yet Manly says of the rhetoricians that "there seems little doubt that Chaucer's character sketches, widely as they later depart from the models offered by the rhetoricians, had their origins in them," and if this is true, then he did not completely throw them off even in the time of his greatest emancipation. Even the absence of rhetorical figures from the fabliau tales

[40] *The Poet Chaucer* (OUP, 1949), 125.
[41] Manly's "Chaucer and the Rhetoricians" was the ground-breaking and enormously seminal study here. "Chaucer's development reveals itself unmistakably, not as progress from crude, untrained power to a style and method polished by fuller acquaintance with rhetorical precepts and more sophisticated models, but rather a process of gradual release from the astonishingly artificial and sophisticated art with which he began and the gradual replacement of formal rhetorical devices by methods of composition based upon close observation of life and the exercise of the creative imagination." See, further, Dorothy Everett, "Some Reflections on Chaucer's 'Art Poetical,' " *Proceedings of the British Academy*, Vol. XXXVI (1950), 131–54. The only conspicuous dissenter from Manly's views is the recent James J. Murphy, "A New Look at Chaucer and the Rhetoricians," *RES*, n.s. Vol. XV (1964), 1–20, who finds in Chaucer only "a layman's consciousness of greater and less complexity in styles, without a rhetorician's knowledge of fine distinctions," which he could easily have acquired at second hand. However this may be, it does not alter the fact that Chaucer's early work conforms to the precepts of the French rhetoricians and that his later work departs from them whenever he chooses to do so or is so compelled by the effects he wishes to secure. The process of emancipation is traced by Agnes K. Getty, "The Mediaeval-Modern Conflict in Chaucer," *PMLA*, Vol. XLVII (1932), 385–402.

was in accord with their precepts, for they forbade "colores" when dealing with undignified materials. On the other hand, if Chaucer never quite threw them off, he had never followed them quite slavishly either. In his French period, says Kittredge, "he was, to all intents and purposes, a French love-poet writing . . . in the English language." But he *did* write in the *English* language, and this a slavish imitator would not have done. Later, when, as scholars say for their own convenience, he passed out of his French into his Italian period, there encountering such great writers as Dante, Petrarch, and Boccaccio,[42] he used them differently than he had used the minor Frenchmen. Both because he was now in surer command of his own instrument and because, being themselves so much greater, they stimulated him profoundly and upon a deeper level, he did not now imitate merely but was stirred to a new creativity; as Kittredge says, "they were his emancipators."

Chaucer's response to and use of the giant of Italian and all medieval writing, Dante, is especially interesting. In view of the tremendous temperamental differences between Chaucer's urbanity and Dante's terrible intensity (to say nothing of their respective subject matter), it is absurd to think of "The House of Fame" or any other work as "Dante in English," as some writers used to do, and one can hardly believe that this point needs to be made at the present time. That Chaucer read Dante with absorption admits of no question however, and as Lowes remarked, he is most likely to remember him when he himself is deeply moved,

> and particularly that passage in which Dante, too, was most profoundly stirred—the sublime prayer of Saint Bernard to Mary with which the last canto of the *Paradiso* opens. It is with one of Dante's majestic invocations that the *Troilus* closes, and, blended with reminiscences of the Bible and of the great hymns from the Service of the Church, Saint Ber-

---

[42] Boccaccio, of course, was the principal influence upon both *Troilus* and "The Knight's Tale." It is not orthodox to credit Chaucer with knowledge of the *Decameron,* and his acquaintance with it has certainly not been proved, but I must say that scholars are not always so scrupulous in crediting sources as they have been here.

nard's prayer again lends grave beauty to the Prologues of the Prioress and the Second Nun.[43]

Chaucer's study of Dante may have contributed something to his own skill as a portraitist, and his meditations on "gentilesse" and on free will and moral responsibility show this influence as well as that of Boethius. The notes in Robinson and in other editions will document the echoes in "The House of Fame," "The Parliament of Fowls," *Troilus and Criseyde*, and elsewhere. Chaucer took the Ugolino material in "The Monk's Tale" direct from the "Inferno," characteristically shifting the emphasis from Dante's horror to his own pity, and his suggestion that the soul of the wicked Sultaness Donegild in "The Man of Law's Tale" inhabited hell even while her body still moved about on earth seems indebted to the "Inferno" also. Chaucer does not always retain Dante's sublimity and high seriousness. The terrible inscription at the entrance to hell which Cary impressively translated as "All hope abandon, ye who enter here"—

> *Per me si va nella città dolente;*
> *Per me si va nell' eterno dolore;*
> *Per me si va tra la perduta gente—*

is echoed at the gate of the "park walled with grene ston" in "The Parliament":

> "Thorgh me men gon into that blysful place
> Of hertes hele and dedly woundes cure;
> Thorgh me men gon into the welle of grace,
> There grene and lusty May shal evere endure.
> This is the wey to al good aventure.
> Be glad, thow redere, and thy sorwe of-caste;
> Al open am I—passe in, and sped thee faste!"[44]

---

[43] John W. Clark, "Dante and the Epilogue of *Troilus*," *JEGP*, Vol. L (1951), 1–10, derives "almost every detail" of the Epilogue from "Paradiso," Cantos XIV and XXII. George Williams suggested also the last twenty lines of "Paradiso" XXV and the first sixty-six lines of "Paradiso" XXVI. See, further, Mary Virginia Rosenfeld, "Chaucer and the Liturgy," *MLN*, Vol. LV (1940), 357–60.

[44] Ll. 127–33.

I hope it is not necessary to explain that such use implies no dis-
respect either toward Dante or toward religion. If it seems so to
the modern sense of reverence (which I doubt), then medieval
men certainly had other ideas about such things.[45] Per contra,
Chaucer was equally capable of using a bit of frivolity in a perfectly
serious context, as when, in "The Parson's Tale" he quotes "thilke
newe Frenshe song, 'Jay tout perdu mon temps et mon labour' "
to illustrate the point that all the good the sinner may do while in
a state of mortal sin is without value in God's sight.[46]

The truth of the matter is that, like many another great writer,
Chaucer read creatively and was often most creative when most
abundantly supplied with "sources." I have already remarked that
this was true both in the Wife of Bath's Prologue and at the beginning of the General Prologue. The Wife herself, in her hetero-
dox argument in behalf of female supremacy, appeals with equal
gusto to authority and to her own experience; in so doing she was
a true daughter of Chaucer. The difference between *The Road to
Xanadu* and thousands of dull-as-ditchwater "source studies" that
have helped bring scholarship into disrepute is that John Livingston Lowes did not stop with *listing* what Coleridge read but
showed how he used it and built up a vivid picture of his mind at
work. And what he did for Coleridge on a gigantic scale in this,
one of the great monuments of American literary scholarship in
its generation, he did in miniature for Chaucer in *Geoffrey
Chaucer and the Development of His Genius* and in the British
Academy lecture, "The Art of Geoffrey Chaucer," which was reprinted in his *Essays in Appreciation*.[47] If you would know how
Chaucer *used* his reading there is no substitute for reading these
works (not that anyone capable of reading Chaucer would wish to
avoid them), for they cannot be summarized. And Lowes was at
his best when he demonstrated that Chaucer's was what he called
"a powerfully associative memory, which played, as he read, over

[45] See Howard Schless, "Chaucer and Dante," in Dorothy Bethurum, ed.,
Critical Approaches to Mediaeval Literature (Col, 1960).
[46] Sister M. Madeleva, *A Lost Language*, 77.
[47] (HM, 1936).

the multitude of impressions from previous reading, with which his mind was stored." The poet's mind "moved like a magnet over his reading, and his recollections fell together like iron-filings into a new, yet to his audience provocatively reminiscent thing."

IV

OF LOVE AND VIRTUE

Discussing Chaucer's attitude toward love involves a number of different general and specific considerations. His sexual frankness needs no arguing; neither is it confined to the fabliau tales. I do not know whether his mention of "stewe" (brothel), without any apparent sign of moral revulsion, when listing the possible causes of dreams at the beginning of "The House of Fame," has any significance or not; after all, "prison" and "gret distresse" are in the same list, and I do not suppose anyone would argue that Chaucer rushed to embrace either of them simply because he mentioned them. He seems pretty coy in indicating Januarie's activities in bed with May and her adultery with Damyan afterwards, but this may have been intended to indicate the vulgarity of the narrator, the Merchant. I do not believe, however, that what the Man of Law says about the bedding of Constance and the Sultan was intended as a dramatic utterance, and certainly there can be no doubt about Chaucer's respect for her.

> They goon to bedde, as it was skile and right;
> For thogh that wyves be ful hooly thynges,

79

They moste take in pacience at nyght
Swich manere necessaries as been plesynges
To folk that han ywedded hem with rynges,
And leye a lite hir holynesse aside,
As for the tyme,—it may no bet bitide.[1]

In other words, Chaucer accepted the universe, and his universe
included sex. I do not believe that innocence in the sense of ignorance ever made much appeal to him, and squeamishness attracted
him even less. At the very outset of his career he tells us of the lady
Whyte in "The Book of the Duchess":

I sey nat that she ne had knowynge
What harm was; or elles she
Had koud no good, so thinketh me,

which is just about what Milton says in the *Areopagitica*.

But Chaucer is far from taking up an amoral point of view, in
sexual or in other matters. "The Pardoner's Tale" involves condemnation of gluttony, drunkenness,[2] gaming, and swearing, and

---

[1] St. Cecilia, in "The Second Nun's Tale," did "bet betide" (if it was "bet").
Did Chaucer, then, believe that women desire sex less than men? Certainly this
would not be true of the wife of Bath or the other Alison in "The Miller's Tale." It
is true of May in her contacts with Januarie, because he is repulsive, and she does
not love him, nor has she reason to, but she is not precisely frigid when she comes to
Damyan. Yet the poet may well have believed women more continent (the man
seeks and the woman grants), and I should say he certainly gives the impression of
believing them more faithful. In "The Manciple's Tale" he writes:

Alle thise ensamples speke I by thise men
That been untrewe, and nothyng by wommen.
For men had evere a likerous appetit
On lower thyng to parfourne hire delit
Than on hir wyves, be they never so faire,
Ne never so trewe, ne so debonaire,
Flesh is so newefangel, with meschaunce,
That we ne konne in nothyng han plesaunce
That sowneth unto vertu any while.

The situation does not inspire these reflections, for the story deals with an unfaithful wife, not an unfaithful husband, and the passage I have quoted immediately follows an account of the behavior of the she-wolf in heat.

[2] Most of Chaucer's references to drinking are incidental and of interest partly
because they are so. The Cook's drunkenness in the Manciple's Prologue is described in as disgusting a manner as possible, and the drunken messenger in "The

in "Lak of Stedfastnesse" the poet complains in his own person of deceit, willfulness, corruption, dissension, conspiracy, falsehood, and covetousness. No reader of the Reeve's Prologue could ever imagine that Chaucer intended him to sympathize with that pilgrim's frustrated sensuality, and in "The Merchant's Tale" another aged sinner, in bed with the fair young wife he has purchased for his legalized prostitution, is made as revolting as possible:

> "It is no fors how longe that we pleye;
> In trewe wedlock coupled be we tweye;

Man of Law's Tale" is compared to a pig. In "The Pardoner's Tale" the "tavern sins" entail tragic consequences, and the fact that the Pardoner is himself a drinker does not weaken the force of the preachment. He is obviously a very effective preacher of the artist-variety, and, as Oscar Wilde once observed, the value of an idea has nothing to do with the sincerity of the man who expresses it. Nothing is said specifically about drinking in the Franklin's complaints concerning his low-minded son, but it is clear that the boy frequents taverns (*CT*, V, ll. 673–94). In "The Summoner's Tale" we may read:

> "A lord is lost, if he be vicius;
> And dronkennesse is eek a foul record
> Of any man, and namely in a lord." (*CT*, III, ll. 2048–50.)

Though the Wife of Bath has no dislike for the bottle, it seems more characteristic of Chaucer that he should record of Canacee:

> She was ful mesurable, as wommen be. (*CT*, V. l. 362.)

Where good women are concerned, he is likely either to say nothing about drinking or else make a point of abstention. Of Griselda we are told that

> Wel ofter of the welle than of the tonne
> She drank, (*CT*, IV, ll. 215–16.)

while as for Virginia,

> Bacus hadde of hir mouth right no maistrie;
> For wyn and youthe dooth Venus encresse,
> As men in fyr wol casten oille or gresse. (*CT*, VI, ll. 58–60.)

Of course I do not mean to suggest that Chaucer advocated total abstinence, which is an ideal that probably had not occurred to many in the fourteenth century; in fact he rather goes out of his way to have Criseyde argue against it:

> "In every thyng, I woot, there lith mesure.
> For though a man forbede dronkenesse,
> He naught forbet that every creature
> Be drynekles for alwey, as I gesse." (*TC*, II, ll. 715–18.)

I would not attempt to draw any conclusions concerning Chaucer's own drinking habits from the foregoing, but that he felt strongly the degradation of drunkenness can hardly be denied.

And blessed be the yok that we been inne,
For in our actes we mowe do no synne.
A man may do no synne with his wyf,
Ne hurte hymselven with his ownee knyf;
For we han leve to pleye us by the lawe."
Thus laboureth he til that the day gan dawe;
And thanne he taketh a sop in fyn clarree,
And upright in his bed thanne sitteth he,
And after that he sang ful loude and cleere,
And kiste hys wyf, and made wantown cheere.
He was al coltissh, ful of ragerye,
And ful of jargon as a flekked pye.
The slakke skyn aboute his nekke shaketh,
Whil that he sang, so chaunteth he and craketh.
But God woot what that May thoughte in hir herte,
Whan she hym saugh up sittynge in his sherte,
In his nyght-cappe, and with his nekke lene;
She preyseth nat his pleyyng worth a bene.

The shift to the woman's point of view at the end here seems to me interesting and remarkable, nor is this the first time it has occurred, for we have already been told that

> he kisseth hire ful ofte;
> With thikke brustles of his berd unsofte,
> Lyk to the skyn of houndfyssh, sharp as brere.

One can almost feel those "thikke brustles," but insofar as one does, one feels with the woman, not the man.

Chaucer accepted sex, then, and no doubt enjoyed it, but he also believed that a man must be able to control it. This, among other things, is what being a man means, for that which is permissible to a beast is not necessarily permissible to him. And Palamon cries:

> "What governance is in this prescience,
> That giltelees tormenteth innocence?
> And yet encresseth this al my penaunce,

That man is bounden to his observaunce,
For Goddes sake, to letten of his wille,
Ther as a beest may al his lust fulfille."[3]

In the Middle Ages writing was not only largely a masculine but even largely a clerical affair, and clerics, being both men and, supposedly at least, ascetics, could hardly have been expected to look at the world through a woman's eyes. Consequently satire of marriage and of women was very common in medieval writing. Chaucer reflects this tradition in many passages, and since he was a humorist, and the joys and sorrows of marriage have always been high on the humorist's list of favorite subjects, he could hardly have been expected to avoid this theme. Good examples would be the "Lenvoy de Chaucer a Bukton" and the "Lenvoy to Scogan." In "The Man of Law's Tale" we are told that women have been the instruments of Satan ever since Eve, and in "The Nun's Priest's Tale" Chaucer records (or permits the narrator to record) Chauntecleer's judgment that he who follows woman's counsel must come to grief and then adds a halfhearted apology. The Wife of Bath sees deceit, weeping, and spinning as God's salient gifts to women, and the whole point of her story—and her prologue—is that women desire mastery in the home above all other things. Women appear as lechers in several of the stories, and after hearing "The Merchant's Tale" the Host generalizes:

"Lo, which sleightes and subtiltees
In wommen been! for ay as bisy as bees
Been they, us sely men for to deceyve."

Both the Host and the Merchant are unhappily married, and the first part of "The Merchant's Tale" is crammed with irony:

A wyf! a, Seinte Marie, *benedicite!*
How myghte a man han any adversitee
That hath a wyf? Certes, I kan nat seye.
The blisse which that is bitwixe hem tweye
Ther may no tonge telle, or herte thynke.

[3] *CT*, I, ll. 1313–18.

The opinion of Theophrastus, that it is cheaper to keep a servant than a wife, is cited, and the narrator adds:

> But take no kep of al swich vanytee;
> Deffie Theofraste, and herke me.

Woman was created for man's help and ardent praise. She is the veritable gift of God, more valuable than lands and rents.

> A wyf wol laste, and in thyn hous endure,
> Wel lenger than thee list, paraventure.

The best argument in favor of the interpretation of such passages as conventional or mischievous or both is that Chaucer does not seem wholly cynical even in "The Merchant's Tale." Almost in the same breath in which he tells of the adultery of May, aided and abetted by Proserpina as the representative of womankind, he expresses his appreciation of

> Wommen ful trewe, ful goode, and vertuous.
> Witnesse on hem that dwelle in Cristes hous;
> With martidom they preved hire constance.

If the satirical praise of marriage in "The Merchant's Tale" is plainly ironical, what he has to say about the reunion of Constance and Alla in "The Man of Law's Tale" seems in dead earnest:

> But finally, whan that the sothe is wist
> That Alla giltelees was of hir wo,
> I trowe an hundred tymes been they kist,
> And swich a blisse is ther bitwix hem two
> That, save the joye that lasteth everemo,
> Ther is noon lyk that any creature
> Hath seyn or shal, whil that the world may dure.

And if there ever was in literature a wife who exemplified the *Ewig-Weibliche* who leads men upward for their good, surely Dame Prudence in "The Tale of Melibee" is such a wife. She may not appeal to many of us, but there can be no doubt concerning either her wisdom or her nobility of character.

Howard Patch remarks rightly that Chaucer's women have charm and that "he seems to notice character even before the loveliness of women." He treats women with respect, and even those who behave badly "have fallen from a level of some importance." (Certainly all his worst rogues are men.) In his early works, and in short poems like "Merciles Beaute," "Womanly Noblesse," and "A Complaint to His Lady," Chaucer presents a conventional chivalric ideal:

> Hir name is Bountee, set in womanhede,
>> Sadnesse in youthe, and Beautee prydelees
>> And Pleasaunce, under governaunce and drede;
> Hir surname is eek Faire Rewthelees,
>> The Wyse, yknit unto Good Aventure.[4]

There are conventional elements, too, in the description of Whyte in "The Book of the Duchess," but this seems much more like a portrait of a real woman, whose physical charms and moral qualities are presented with equal relish. But from here on the poet moves steadily in the direction of realism, or, better, reality. Criseyde is individualized physically by such touches as the joining of her eyebrows and her wearing her hair down her back, unbound save by a thread of gold. And we are told of Alison in "The Miller's Tale" that her brows were "smale ypulled," and that her forehead shone as bright as day,

> So was it wasshen when she leet hir werk.

Chaucer seems wholly sincere in his appreciation of saintly women like Constance in "The Man of Law's Tale" and Virginia in "The Physician's Tale." (St. Cecilia, I think, never quite comes to life.) But he surely did not confine his appreciation to such women. Surely he loved Dido, both in "The House of Fame" and in *The Legend of Good Women*; he was so completely in her corner that he was willing to blacken Aeneas by playing down his mission and thus making his desertion of her the more reprehensible. But go back for a moment to Alison. Surely she is one of

---

[4] "A Complaint to His Lady," ll. 24–29.

the most "likerous" women in literature. Chaucer had no illusions about her; in his stimulating description of her when she is first introduced all his comparisons are with animals and the things of the earth, and there is no suggestion of spirit. But he is careful to withhold any suggestion of grossness, reserving that for the denouement, where he serves it up in heaping measure. Meanwhile he was not enough of a hypocrite to pretend that she did not attract him and not enough of a Pharisee to cast the first stone at her. He never sneers at her. (Are her devotions at the parish church satirically presented? I see no reason to suppose so.) "Chaucer saw her as a fine product of nature," says Patch (and it could not be said better), "and any touch of perfection moved him; just so he might have described the pear tree itself or the ripe apple."

Griselda in "The Clerk's Tale" is different. She, too, is a saint, but unlike Constance and Virginia, she is a saint in whose god Chaucer did not believe. Neither did he expect his readers to do so.[5]

> This storie is seyd, nat for that wyves sholde
> Folwen Grisilde as in humylitee,
> For it were inportable, though they wolde;
> But for that every wight, in his degree,
> Sholde be constant in adversitee
> As was Grisilde; therfore Petrak writeth
> This storie, which with heigh stile he enditeth.

We may suspect a touch of irony here, for surely the references which follow to

> the Wyves love of Bathe—
> Whos lyf and al hire secte God mayntene

and the "archewyves" cannot have been made with quite a straight face. Yet Chaucer does not misrepresent Petrarch, for he himself had made the religious application.

Our difficulties with "The Clerk's Tale" probably stem ulti-

---

[5] In fact, nobody ever has except Percy Van Dyke Shelly, who makes the amazing statements (*The Living Chaucer*, 276) that "Walter is at bottom an ideal husband and father" and that he acts "within the bounds of the natural and the human"!

mately from the fact, developed by D. D. Griffith and others,[6] that in the original form of the story Walter was an otherworldly being, like Cupid in the Cupid and Psyche tale or like Lohengrin, but they have been greatly increased by the medieval tendency to develop characters only in relationship to the central theme of the story and to omit or gloss over other traits, with almost complete indifference to the ideal of well-rounded characterization which moderns cherish. For this reason our tendency to worry over whether Griselda was or was not a good mother, or whether she performed her duty toward her children when she permitted Walter to take them away from her and, as she supposed, destroy them, are quite beside the point, for "The Clerk's Tale" deals with Griselda not as mother but as wife, and what kind of a mother she was would be, as Kipling says, "another story." Such problems always arise when old stories are recharactered or supernatural material rationalized, and those who wish their literature always to be entirely reasonable and consistent had better leave such things alone. Moreover, Chaucer must certainly have distinguished, as we do, between what he could admire in literature and what he admired in life; our literary sympathies are always much wider. We accept Hamlet's fundamental nobility of character, though we could not believe that we ourselves had the right to avenge a murder, and we sympathize wholly with Romeo and Juliet when they kill themselves for love but fail to sympathize at all, however we may pity them, with a pair of young fools whose identical act is reported in the morning paper. For Romeo and Juliet are characters in a love tragedy. Their sole duty is to be faithful unto death, and they perform it nobly. But real people have—or should have—many other obligations and interests. Thus I do not believe that Chaucer had any difficulty in at once admiring Griselda and deploring the situation in which she was placed.

Chaucer's greatest characterizations of women are unquestionably Criseyde and the Wife of Bath, and the consideration of each

---

[6] "The Origin of the Griselda Story," *University of Washington Publications in Language and Literature*, Vol. VIII (1931). See also Robinson's note on "The Clerk's Tale," pp. 709–10 of his edition.

involves special topics. Rejecting Boccaccio's somewhat lusty heroine of the *Filostrato*—and never even considering the possibility of the wanton Shakespeare drew after her legend had been debased through two more centuries—Chaucer created in Criseyde a thoroughly charming woman, himself fell in love with her, and found himself in something of a quandary when he was obliged to describe her infidelity. Like Manon Lescaut, Criseyde is capable of loving a man and betraying him at the same time, but she is considerably less shallow and self-seeking, and she is also much less of what is called in the theater an ingénue. An affectionate woman, and emphatically of "the marrying kind," she is not easily won, and we are obviously intended to take her statement of why she yielded to Troilus at face value:

> "For trusteth wel, that your estat roial,
> Ne veyn delit, nor only worthinesse
> Of yow in werre or torney marcial,
> Ne pompe, array, nobleye, or ek richesse
> Ne made me to rewe on youre destresse;
> But moral vertu, grounded upon trouthe,
> That was the cause I first hadde on yow routhe!
>
> "Eke gentil herte and manhod that ye hadde,
> And that ye hadde, as me thoughte, in despit
> Every thyng that souned into badde,
> As rudenesse and poeplish appetit,
> And that your resoun bridlede youre delit;
> This made, aboven every creature,
> That I was youre, and shal while I may dure."[7]

When we meet her, she is a blameless widow, and such she would have remained had it rested with her to take any initiative to alter her estate. If her love gives only in response to desire, then the more woman she, and there is no suggestion at any point that she loves Troilus less than he loves her (though she may well love him less tempestuously), or that theirs would not have been a permanent union had not outside circumstances interfered.

[7] *TC*, IV, ll. 1667–80.

But Criseyde is like many women—even good women—in that convention means more to her than principle, and she plays the courtly love game so strictly according to the rules that some time must pass before she can admit even to herself that she wants just what her lover wants. Her compromising spirit appears clearly as soon as the proposition comes to send her out of Troy. Her arguments for compliance, "sensible" as they are, and perhaps all the more so because they are sensible, all seem pretty tame, and though she is quite as "sincere" in her love as Troilus, she will not fight to hold it, nor kick against the pricks as he does when threatened with its destruction. There is even a touch of cynicism about her:

> "My fader, as ye knowen wel, parde,
> Is old, and elde is ful of coveytise;
> And I right now have founden al the gise,
> Withouten net, wherewith I shal hym hente.
> And herkeneth now, if that ye wol assente."[8]

Here, as later with Diomede, she is making terms with life, as Troilus cannot do it. Now, she even tells herself, as she is telling him, that her absence will be only temporary; then, much more pitifully, she will spread the compost on the weeds, promising herself that, having failed her true lover, she will at least be true to the oaf who has replaced him. (There would be no possibility of deceiving him, nor, unfortunately, does he deserve fidelity.) But if all this is characteristically feminine, perhaps it is only on some such terms that woman has been able to survive in a man's world.

Chaucer loved her, but he will not lie for her. She "falsed" Troilus, but that is no reason why he should "falsen" his "matere." His attitude toward her is a model of Christian charity, and if all men were like him today, every scandal sheet in the world would go out of business tomorrow.[9] In the Prologue to *The Legend of Good*

[8] *TC*, IV, ll. 1368–72.
[9] Criseyde is not the only woman to profit by Chaucer's charity. In the "Hercules" tragedy in "The Monk's Tale" Chaucer must report his death of a poisoned shirt furnished by Dianira, his wife. Then he adds, characteristically,

> But nathelees somme clerkes hire excusen
> By oon that highte Nessus, that it maked.
> Be as by may, I wol hire noght accusen.

Women, where he is accused of having blasphemed against love by writing of Criseyde, he tells us specifically what he was trying to achieve:

> "Algate, God wot, it was myn entente
> To forthere trouthe in love and it cheryce,
> And to be war fro falsnesse and fro vice
> By swich ensample; this was my menynge."[10]

He suffers with her in her fall and refuses to be her judge. Because he refuses to view the weaknesses of the human heart without sympathy he keeps himself free of what Hawthorne thought the unpardonable sin. "Men seyn—I not" that Criseyde was false. Chaucer can't go against "the books" any more than Tom Sawyer could. But his feelings are his own affair.

> Allas! that they sholde evere cause fynde
> To speke hire harm, and if they on hire lye,
> Iwis, hemself sholde han the vilanye.[11]

And he beseeches "every gentil womman" who reads him

> That al be that Criseyde was untrewe,
> That for that gilt she be nat wroth with me.
> Ye may hire giltes in other bokes se;
> And gladlier I wol write, yif yow leste,
> Penelopeës trouthe and good Alceste.[12]

Yet, for all that, she is a sustained characterization—one woman, not two—and the commentators who see Chaucer describing an ideal heroine in the first three books and then simply throwing up the sponge when he comes to the inherited intractable element of the betrayal have not read very carefully. I have called her a "marrying" woman, yet she does not marry Troilus, nor is the possibility of marriage between them ever discussed. If the *Troilus* was intended to be read as a court-of-love poem, then Criseyde incurred no fault in yielding to Troilus but only in betraying him,

[10] G, ll. 461–64.
[11] TC, IV, ll. 19–21.
[12] TC, V, ll. 1774–78.

though it is a little startling to find so distinctively Christian a writer as C. S. Lewis saying flatly that "she commits no unpardonable sin against any code I know of—unless, perhaps, against that of the Hindus."[13] But none of this really has much to do with Chaucer's fundamental conception of Criseyde's character. He saw her as "slyding of corage" and the most fearful creature that ever was, but, for all her charm, I do not see how it can be denied that he saw her also as a worldly woman. In a mild way, she was a skeptic too, and this is not an unimportant element in her characterization, for, like Spenser, Chaucer knew that Sansloy treads upon the heels of Sansfoy. She is not the stuff of which martyrs are made, and she could no more be one of Cupid's saints than Christ's; we need only compare her with Constance, Virginia, or Griselda to be sure of that. You and I may prefer her to these other women; there is no law about preferences, but we should remember that autobiography is not criticism. Under comfortable conditions, Criseyde could never have soiled her name nor broken her lover's heart. It was her tragedy that she was not called upon to live her life under comfortable conditions, and, judged as a spiritual being, she made it worse by making herself as comfortable as possible under bad conditions, and losing her life to find it.

But is *Troilus and Crisede* a courtly love poem? and can Chaucer be called a courtly love poet? I do not believe that either question can be answered with a simple "yes" or "no."

He certainly used court-of-love conventions in his earlier poetry,

[13] *The Allegory of Love* (OUP, 1936). It is only fair to add, however, that Lewis goes on to qualify. Chesterton found in the ending of the *Troilus* an expression of Chaucer's conviction "that happiness is not to be found by dancing after any heathen god of love; but by looking up . . . to where a more terrible but a more tender god of love hangs, not on Olympus but on Calvary." "That is to say," comments Paull F. Baum, "Troilus, son of the King of Troy, should have delayed a few centuries, until after the Crucifixion: he should simply not have been a pagan, for no pagan can find happiness." *Chaucer, A Critical Appreciation* (Duke University Press, 1958). The comment is not very penetrating, since all Chesterton is saying is that Christianity has an answer to the human problem which is not to be found in paganism. That much any Christian critic is bound to keep in mind, and even critics who are not Christians would do well to do so when interpreting Christian writers. Chaucer does show, as we shall see in the next chapter, that he was aware of Troilus and Criseyde suffering under disadvantages because they were pagans.

and this regardless of whether the "eight-year sickness" referred to in the "The Book of the Duchess" had autobiographical significance or not.[14] The "hereos" or lovesickness of Palamon and Arcite is quite according to form, and both are presented as very "manly" young men. In "The Man of Law's Tale" even the Sultan suffers from hereos. In *The Legend of Good Women*, Theseus, though a king's son, offers Ariadne

> in low manere
> To ben youre page and serven yow ryght here.

And in the *Legend* Prologue, Alceste tells the God of Love concerning Chaucer himself that

> While he was yong, he kept youre estat;
> I not wher he be now a renegat,

and goes on to credit the poet with

> many an ympne for your halydayes,
> That highten balades, roundeles, vyrelayes.

From another point of view, Chaucer himself speaks in his Retraction of "many a song and many a lecherous lay," and Gower too tells us that

> in the floure of his youthe
> In sondri wise, as he wel couthe,
> Of ditees and of songes glade,
> The which he for mi [Venus'] sake made,
> The lond fulfild is overal.

Courtly love was never anything but an upper-class ideal, and it is difficult to tell to what extent it was even here more than a literary convention. It conflicted with Christian ethics in sanctioning sexual intercourse outside of marriage, but it was by no means amoral in its outlook. The prescription of secrecy may have been determined basically by the consideration that under the

14 The views on this subject are summarized by J. Burke Severs, "Chaucer's Self-Portrait in 'The Book of the Duchess,' " *PQ*, Vol. XLIII (1964), 27–39. See, further, Lewis, *The Allegory of Love*, and E. E. Slaughter, *Virtue According to Love—in Chaucer* (Bookman Associates, 1957).

system one's beloved was very likely to be another man's wife, but it also involved the idea that love was too sacred to be profaned by disclosure. Courtly love involved fidelity, personal devotion, and, on the lover's side, obedience, and there is no reason to suppose that it placed a heavier stress upon sensuality than marriage itself. Moreover, under the medieval system of making marriage an affair of barter and arrangement even in childhood —and this by no means only among royalty and nobility—it could only be by accident that a man might be in love with his wife or a woman with her husband,[15] and it might not unreasonably be argued that it was the marriage system that really debauched medieval morals and the court-of-love code which nurtured such idealism in sexual matters as managed to stay alive. It is a mistake to suppose that court-of-love ideas have wholly died out in modern times. Robert Louis Stevenson expressed the opinion that some of the ugliest adulteries are committed in the bed of marriage and under the sanction of religion and law (it is part of Januarie's degradation in "The Merchant's Tale" that he cannot understand this), and surely all decent people feel only contempt for the man who will, as the saying is, "kiss and tell."[16]

It is true that Chaucer seems to describe the love raptures of Troilus and Criseyde with complete sympathy:

> O blisful nyght, of hem so longe isought,
> How blithe unto hem bothe two thow weere!
> Why nad I swich oon with my soule ybought,
> Ye, or the leeste joie that was theere?
> Awey, thow foule daunger and thow feere,

[15] See Coulton, *Chaucer and His England*—Chapter XVI, "Husbands at the Church Door."

[16] See the "Envoy" to J. A. W. Bennett, *"The Parlement of Foules": An Interpretation* (OUP, 1957), for an eloquent tribute to the French poets searching "for a meeting-place between ethics, passion, and traditional teaching," and in the course of the quest finding "new paths for the human spirit. If some of them strayed from orthodox doctrine, some of them enlarged the boundaries of Christian thought on love and marriage; and if their paths issue in no earthly paradise, they lead—or Chaucer's do—to that special kind of *Canterbury Tales* contentment wherein, having seen all varieties of human folly and self-deception, we come to an abiding sense of the worth and purpose of human love, even though we be no whit the nearer to defining or explaining it."

And lat them in this hevene blisse dwelle,
That is so heigh that al ne kan I telle!

But is it not also true that we learn only from the context that Troilus and Criseyde are not married? Neither one belongs to anybody else, and there is nothing in either their conduct or their feelings toward each other that would have to be changed if they were married. To borrow a distinction from Milton this is sex on a high level of human dignity, not the hasty "casual fruition" which he associated with harlots and saw Adam and Eve indulging in after the fall.

To all intents and purposes, in other words, Criseyde *is* the *wife* of Troilus, and that is why her infidelity is terrible. In *The Legend of Good Women* Chaucer insists too that Dido and Hypsipyle and Ariadne are wives; even Cleopatra is Antony's wife, as Milton, quite unbiblically, made Dalila Samson's wife. In both "The Wife of Bath's Tale" and "The Franklin's Tale" love exists in marriage, which was not according to the courtly love way of thinking:

Arveragus and Dorigen his wyf
In sovereyn blisse leden forth hir lyf.
Nevere eft ne was ther angre hem bitwene.
He cherisseth hire as though she were a queene,
And she was to hym trewe for everemoore.[17]

And, as Chesterton remarked, Chaucer's ideal woman is Alcestis, the very arch-type of faithful wifehood. Patch is a little startling but he is not unreasonable when he suggests that there may have been, as the saying is, more truth than poetry, and more truth than humor too, "in the accusation that Chaucer was an enemy to love, that is, if we mean love *paramours*."

But what, now, of the Wife of Bath? If Christ did not "speak

[17] George R. Coffman, "Chaucer and Courtly Love Once More," *Speculum*, Vol. XX (1945), 43–50, is apropos here. Agnes K. Getty, "Chaucer's Conception of the Humble Lover," *PMLA*, Vol. XLIV (1929), 200–19, sees Chaucer moving away from the conventional court-of-love conception from "The House of Fame" on. See, further, Gervaise Mathew, "Marriage and Amour Courtois in Late-Fourteenth Century England," *Essays Presented to Charles Williams* (OUP, 1947).

himself broad" in Holy Writ, she certainly spoke herself broad in what Chaucer writ, and from the point of view of genteel standards, there *was* "vilyenye" in it, but there was no offense against either art or morals. The first great shaded and elaborated character in English literature, she can be matched in her particular brand of earthy vitality only by Falstaff and Mrs. Gamp. And all three are such marvelously entertaining rascals that readers often overlook their more unsavory qualities. But Chaucer was not confused (nor Shakespeare nor Dickens neither), though Chaucer was fascinated by the Wife to the extent of giving her a Prologue to her tale out of all proportion to what he gave the others; indeed it is almost as long as the General Prologue itself. As to morals, David Holbrook may be somewhat romantic when he tells us that "Chaucer, through the Wyf of Bath, gives us . . . acceptance [of sex], in comedy, but with the humane purpose of accepting one reality before going on to explore a greater which transcends it, and yet proves more real," but he is right in perceiving her marvelous vitality as "totally subject to Time, decline, and Death" and therefore painfully aware of mortality. He notes further, as others have noted, that though she has been married five times, she says nothing about children, so that it looks very much as though for her, sex had been barren.[18] In one respect, too, she was just plain unfortunate: the only husband she really loved was the one she could not control, and he abused her.

Like all who have lived sensual lives primarily, the Wife finds growing old a tragedy. As Manly has told us, her headdress is a generation out of date, and for her who boasted that she was never without "purveiaunce" in marriage, the lusty succession at last has failed. Husband #5 is dead, but Husband #6 is not knocking at the door, and probably will not knock. It may even be that she has gone on the pilgrimage to find him, and that her audacious Prologue is a frank setting-forth of her wares.

> "But, Lord Crist! whan that it remembreth me
> Upon my yowthe, and on my jolitee,

18 *The Quest for Love* (University of Alabama Press, 1966).

95

It tikleth me aboute myn herte roote.
Unto this day it dooth myn herte boote
That I have had my world as in my tyme."

This is one of the great dramatic utterances of literature, but surely it is also very sad. "Remembreth," "have had," "as in my tyme"—these are the key words. The good time is past, and it never will come again.

Yet she is not quite like Falstaff or Mrs. Gamp, for she is much more respectable than either. She is a working woman and an artisan—

Of clooth-makyng she hadde swich an haunt,
She passed hem of Ypres and of Gaunt—

and she maintained her standing in the community, as neither of the others did:

She was a worthy womman al hir lyve.

Falstaff, to be sure, is a knight, and Mrs. Gamp is a nurse. But Falstaff goes to war not to fight but to play possum and flourish a bottle instead of a pistol, and Mrs. Gamp goes nursing to put her mouth to the bottle "on the chimley piece" and to steal her patient's pillow because her easy chair is "harder than a brick-badge."

We cannot even be sure that the Wife has committed adultery, though she has certainly fornicated:

Housbondes at chirche dore she hadde fyve,
Withouten oother compaignye in youthe.

The "compaignye" was carnal, surely, but this was before she was married. In certain passages she seems to suggest that she claimed extramarital freedom for herself, and she certainly flirted with Jankyn while his predecessor was still alive, but there is at least one passage in which she specifically denies adultery:

"Now wol I tellen of my fourthe housbonde.
I seye, I hadde in herte greet despit

96

That he of any oother had delit.
But he had quit, by God and by Seint Joce!
I made hym of the same wode a croce;
Nat of my body, in no foul manere,
But certeinly, I made folk swich cheere
That in his owene grece I made hym frye
For angre, and for verray jalousye."

It may be, as John Speirs suggests,[19] that the Wife's temperamental affinity is with the nature-cults or "fayerye" which she refers to so boldly and so charmingly at the beginning of her tale, but if so it is only her desires which are pagan; her mind has never questioned the fundamental Christian values.

"Allas! allas! that evere love was synne!"

It is a cry which, as Lowes has remarked, "sums up half the passion and pain of the world," and nobody has said more. But it has meaning only for those who inherit the Jewish-Christian ethic. For pagans love was never "synne." As the Reverend Mr. Davidson's wife points out in Colton and Randolph's *Rain*, when she and her husband went to the South Seas as missionaries, they had to "teach" the natives "what sin is."

The Wife hates virginity, yet she accepts the basic medieval notion that it is nobler than sexuality. She has read and pondered with some intelligence and discrimination what the Bible has to say about sex and marriage, and she has no doubts concerning any of the basic Christian doctrines. Her fundamental, unanswerable objection to virginity—that if all women were content to remain virgins, there could be no more virgins—echoes St. Jerome, and she is quite in harmony with St. Thomas Aquinas and Catholic teaching in general that continence is not required of all.[20] She distinguishes sharply between what is commanded of Christians and what is only suggested as a counsel of perfection, and she ignores the latter because, as she says frankly, per-

[19] *Chaucer the Maker* (Faber and Faber, 1941).
[20] See, on this point, Dorothy Bethurum's valuable discussion in "Chaucer's Point of View as Narrator," *PMLA*, Vol. LXXIV (1959), especially pp. 518–19.

fection does not appeal to her, but she neither denies its possibility for others nor despises it in them. There is even an attractive element of Christian humility in her attitude toward herself on this point. You may have gold dishes in your house, she says, but you do not use them every day, for you have wooden dishes too, and these have their use and value. In another passage, she herself is hot barley bread, set over against the pure wheat of the virgins. It should be noted, also, that she has a horror of perverted sexuality which matches that expressed, for whatever reason, by the Man of Law in his Introduction,[21] and this, I would venture to guess, Chaucer himself shared.

Yet in spite of all that can be said in her favor, the Wife remains a sinner and a very grave one. By medieval standards she sins in her excessive concupiscence,[22] and even if we are disposed to regard this as a slight fault, she must still be called guilty of other sins which seem no less deadly now than they did in the fourteenth century. In a way, she does not even deserve much credit for her view of herself as common clay. She liked common clay and aspired to nothing higher. On the plane where she lived, and wished to live, nobody was more given to pride. Even when she went to the altar for alms and oblations, she had to be first, and if anyone got in ahead of her,

> certeyn so wrooth was she,
> That she was out of alle charitee.

Her "unbuxomness" in marriage is quite in line with this, and she was not honest enough to rise to the level of the prostitute who lives up to her contract and gives service for value received. To

[21] CT, II, 733-36.

[22] E. E. Slaughter, "Allas! allas! that ever love was sinne," MLN, Vol. XLIX (1934), 83-86, explores the tendency of some ecclesiastical writers to enjoin continence even upon married couples while others restrict intercourse to purposes of procreation. In "The Monk's Tale" the pagan Cenobia follows the second group, and the excessive modesty attributed to Julius Caesar (which quite matches that of Lucrece in the Legend) seems equally inappropriate. The Wife had surely read enough in her husband's books to be familiar with these views, but it seems unlikely that Chaucer could have expected his readers to recall and apply all the Scriptural and exegetical associations which D. W. Robertson, Jr., expounds in A Preface to Chaucer, pp. 318ff.

the Wife of Bath sex was not only an indulgence; it was—which is much worse—a weapon. By her own account she "used" her husbands and her own sexuality besides, and once she had got her hands on their property, she felt no further obligation to pay the debt of her flesh to them.

> Deceite, wepyng, spynnyng God hath yive
> To wommen kyndely, whil that they may lyve.
> And thus of o thyng I avaunte me,
> Atte ende I hadde the bettre in ech degree,
> By sleighte, or force, or by som maner thyng,
> As by continueel murmur or grucchyng,
> Namely abedde hadden they meschaunce:
> Ther wolde I chide, and do hem no plesaunce;
> I wolde no lenger in the bed abyde,
> If that I felte his arm over my syde,
> Til he had maad his raunson unto me;
> Thanne wolde I suffre hym to do his nycetee.
> And therfore every man this tale I telle,
> Wynne whoso may, for al is for to selle;
> With empty hand men may none haukes lure.

What I am saying, of course, is that Chaucer knew all the faults and virtues of the Wife of Bath and that his point of view in portraying her is always unmistakably that of a Christian and Catholic writer.

Many years ago, George Lyman Kittredge argued persuasively that the Wife of Bath, in her Prologue and Tale, inaugurated a "marriage group" in *The Canterbury Tales*, in which, to put it briefly, the Wife of Bath opposed the orthodox view of her time that the husband was the head of the house, the Clerk reaffirmed the traditional view by telling the story of patient Griselda, and the Franklin, after interruptions, had the honor of concluding the debate with a tale expressing Chaucer's own ideal, according to which neither party dominates the other but both work together in perfect harmony and co-operation. This argument stated so attractively what modern readers would like

99

to think Chaucer believed that in spite of Henry Barrett Hinckley's vigorous counterblast and the later modifications introduced by such believers as W. W. Lawrence,[23] Chaucer scholars often refer to it as if it were an established fact rather than merely a not unreasonable theory. Theory it remains nevertheless, and there are difficulties in the way of accepting it.

Since the Wife is referred to at the end of "The Clerk's Tale," it is reasonable to suppose that her tale and that of the Clerk were, in some sense, intended to be juxtaposed, but that "The Franklin's Tale" says what Kittredge wished it to say, or that if it does, the Franklin must be thought of as having borrowed Chaucer's voice to say it—all this seems very doubtful. Essentially "The Franklin's Tale" does not concern domination in marriage but the sanctity of the pledged word.[24] Furthermore, Arveragus is not always so considerate of Dorigen as those who view him as an ideal husband (from the modern point of view) would have us believe. He deliberately thrust her in the way of danger when he

> Shoop hym to goon and dwelle a yeer or tweyne
> In Engelond, that cleped was eek Briteyne,
> To seke in armes worshipe and honour;
> For al his lust he sette in swich labour,

[23] Kittredge's "Chaucer's Discussion of Marriage," *MP*, Vol. IX (1911–12), 435–67, and Hinckley's "The Debate on Marriage in *The Canterbury Tales*," *PMLA*, Vol. XXXII (1917), 292–305, are both reprinted in Wagenknecht, *Chaucer: Modern Essays in Criticism*, where see also James Sledd," " 'The Clerk's Tale': The Monsters and the Critics," reprinted from *MP*, Vol. LI (1953), 73–82. For Lawrence, see "The Marriage Group in *The Canterbury Tales*," *MP*, Vol. XI (1913), 247–58, and his book, *Chaucer and The Canterbury Tales* (Col, 1950).

[24] Which, of course, is treated with quite absurd and unbelievable quixotism, both because it is perfectly clear that Dorigen did not intend to be taken literally when she set up what she regarded as an impossible condition before her would-be seducer—

"For wel I woot that it shal never bityde"—

and also because he had not really met the condition, which is to say that the rocks had not actually been removed. Robinson's note on V, l. 1479—

"Trouthe is the hyeste thyng that man may kepe"—

reads, "This is the first moral of the tale." (For that matter, Griselda's pledged word is an important element in "The Clerk's Tale" also; see *CT*, IV, ll. 358–64).

which surely makes him a considerably better knight than husband. More to the point, however, is the utter absence of the freedom from domination in marriage that Kittredge prized which
appears when he learns of the rash promise which his wife had
made. He does not *discuss* the matter with her at all. He simply
commands her to keep her word and *threatens her with death*
should she violate the conditions he has laid down!

> This housbonde, with glad chiere, in freendly wyse
> Answerde and seyde as I shal yow devyse:
> "Is ther oght elles, Dorigen, but this?"
> "Nay, nay," quod she, "God helpe me so as wys!
> This is to muche, and it were Goddes wille."
> "Ye wyf," quod he, "lat slepen that is stille.
> It may be wel, paraventure, yet to day.
> Ye shul youre trouthe holden, by my fay!
> For God so wisly have mercy upon me,
> I hadde wel levere ystiked for to be.
> For verray love which that I to yow have,
> But if ye sholde youre trouthe kepe and save.
> Trouthe is the hyeste thyng that man may kepe"—
> But with that word he brast anon to wepe.
> And seyde, "I vow forbede, up peyne of deeth,
> That nevere, while thee lasteth lyf ne breeth,
> To no wight telle thou of this aventure,—
> As I may best, I wol my wo endure,—
> Ne make no countenance of hevynesse,
> That folke of yow may demen harm or gese."[25]

[25] As others have anticipated me in pointing out, the tales which Kittredge
placed in his "marriage group" are not the only ones in which the problems of
matrimony are involved. One cannot go far in dealing with human life without
involving all the basic institutions and motives; this is, of course, the reason why
Frederick Tuper's attempt to impose a sin-framework on *The Canterbury Tales*
was so unconvincing. See his "Chaucer and the Seven Deadly Sins," *PMLA*, Vol.
XXIX (1914), 93–128, and the reply by John Livingston Lowes under the same
title, *PMLA*, Vol. XXX (1915), 153–63. I have sometimes frivolously suggested
to classes that perhaps Chaucer intended "The Second Nun's Tale," in which
St. Cecilia's marriage is never consummated, to present his solution of the marriage
"problem," but I never expected to find this seriously argued, as, in a sense, it is

I do not know what Chaucer believed about "maistrye" in marriage. As I have already indicated, I do not believe that he possessed a doctrinaire kind of mind, and he may well never have considered the question in the terms which Kittredge postulated. But I am sure that here, as in any other area, his natural temperamental bent would have been toward moderation. When the formel at the end of "The Parliament of Fowls" asked and received the boon of a year's respite and her "choys al fre," she certainly got more than medieval females in general received from either nature or society, but this may have been determined by the needs of the situation which Chaucer was allegorizing (if there was such a situation). Nevertheless I see no indication that he found it out of order, and I do not believe that he would have done so. I should guess that in his sympathy for women and children too he was abreast of the best thinking of his time or even ahead of it.

> Of alle tresons sovereyn pestilence
> Is whan a wight betrayseth innocence.[26]

Discount the *Legend* if you like on the ground that denunciation of false lovers could not have been avoided here, though surely they did not need to be denounced even in the Thisbe story, where boy and girl are equally faithful. But Chaucer strikes the same note elsewhere. None of his comments on his characters seem to be more sincere or to come from greater depths in him than the passages he added to Trivet expressing his heartfelt sympathy for Constance in "The Man of Law's Tale" and his indignation against those who misuse her, nor is his denunciation of the lustful steward who would violate her necessarily less deeply felt for having been taken from *De Contemptu Mundi*:

by Donald R. Howard, "The Conclusion of the Marriage Group: Chaucer and the Human Condition," *MP*, Vol. LVII (1960), 223–32: "Augustine held up the chaste marriage of the Virgin Mary as an example of the manner in which persons can live perfectly." Mr. Howard, whose article must be read to be appreciated, is not dogmatic, and he is excellent on the balance in Chaucer between the sacred and the secular outlook. He also points out, importantly, I believe, that "The Franklin's Tale" is not in harmony with what the Parson says about proper relations between husband and wife.

[26] *CT*, VI, ll. 91–92 ("The Physicians' Tale").

O foule lust of luxurie, lo, thyn ende!
Nat oonly that thou feyntest mannes mynde,
But verraily thou wolt his body shende.
Th' ende of thy werk, or of thy lustes blynde,
Is compleynyng. Hou many oon may men fynde
That noght for werk somtyme, but for th'entente
To doon this synne, been outher slayn or shente!

The Host's remarks after hearing Virginia's tragedy rehearsed by the Physician may well be, as Lowes says, "the most engaging embodiment I know of the attitude of a typical audience at melodrama," but surely Chaucer intends his readers to sympathize with him. Harry Bailly may be a rough man but when he confronts such an outrage his instincts are right, and this is intended to bring us a certain reassurance as to the fundamental decency of common humanity, just as, for that matter, "the attitude of a typical audience at melodrama" does.

As for children specifically, Chaucer is much more successful in portraying them than Shakespeare was, especially in "The Prioress's Tale." It is no wonder that nineteenth-century critics were tempted to attribute childlikeness of character to the writer himself. The tenderness of Constance and Griselda toward their children is moving, and it cannot be accounted for by reference to the poet's sources. It may seem strange that he threw away an opportunity for pathos in "The Manciple's Tale" by omitting Ovid's touch about the plea of Coronis to Phoebus not to slay her unborn child, but perhaps he thought this would make the unfaithful wife too sympathetic for his purpose. Whether the "lyte Lowys my son" of the "Astrolabe" was Chaucer's own child or not (there *was* a Lewis Chaucer), nobody can deny that there is real tenderness in the way he addresses him.[27]

[27] D. S. Brewer, "Children in Chaucer," *Review of English Literature*, Vol. V (1964), 52–60, finds Chaucer notable among English writers of any period before the nineteenth century for the affectionate love and pity, sometimes verging upon sentimentality, with which he presents babies and children. But though Brewer thinks love of children "one of the orthodoxies of human nature which Chaucer took for granted," he finds him writing always from the adult's point of view, not from that of a child, as Dickens, Mark Twain, and so many others were to do in

Though I do not recall that he ever refers to it, there can hardly have been any passages in the New Testament by which Chaucer was more impressed than Mark 9:42, which contains the solemn warning of Jesus that a very heavy responsibility must be incurred by anyone who causes a "little one" to "offend." "It were better for him that a millstone were hanged about his neck, and he were cast into the sea." Apparently Chaucer felt that a heavy obligation rested upon all decent people to set a good example to children and to guard them against the danger of worldliness. "Feestes, revels, and . . . daunces" become "occasions of dailaunces," and

> maken children for to be
> To soone rype and boold, as men may se,
> Which is ful perilous, and hath been yoore.
> For al to soone may she lerne loore
> Of boldnesse, whan she woxen is a wyf.

And so he interrupts "The Physician's Tale" with a long and solemn address to both parents and guardians, warning them that if any moral harm comes to their charges through their own wickedness or carelessness, they will be held to a strict accountability for it.

> Beth war, that by ensample of youre lyvynge,
> Or by your necligence in chastisynge,
> That they no perisse; for I dar wel seye,
> If that they doon, ye shul it deere abeye.
> Under a shepherde softe and necligent
> The wolf hath many a sheep and lamb torent.

Attempts have been made to explain Chaucer's concern here by reference to the Elizabeth of Lancaster scandal in the family of John of Gaunt and also to the abduction of Isabella atte Halle

---

the nineteenth century. The father-daughter relationship is more tenderly treated than the father-son relationship, but the father-image is always authoritative and sometimes even harsh. The death of children, though mourned, is accepted as a normal thing, as it was and had to be in Chaucer's world, where the infant mortality rate was extremely high. Brewer also cites CT, X, ll. 669–72 as an anecdote for fathers surpassing anything in Wordsworth.

in 1387, the inquiry into which he officially attended. But if he had not accepted the general principle stated, individual violations could not have disturbed him greatly.[28]

I have spoken of Chaucer as a poet of love, but I have so far said nothing about him as an individual lover or husband, and I do not know that there is very much to say. His numerous declarations that he has had no experience in love are, upon any hypothesis, puzzling, and all the more so when we remember that he was writing for a semiprivate audience to much of which both he and his wife were personally known. That there is some kind of joke here is obvious, and probably Chaucer's contemporaries understood it. But that is more than I do, and so far as I have been able to discover none of my contemporaries do either.[29]

This of course leaves the field wide open to conjecture, and nobody can complain that it has gone unoccupied. Is there a wilder or more ridiculous statement in all criticism, I wonder, than John Masefield's "We gather from the poems that Chaucer's own marriage was one of the utmost and liveliest unfortunate horror"? Yes, there is, but Masefield need not fear for his laurels, for he himself has supplied it:

> The Wife of Bath describes her fifth marriage as being to much such a Clerk as Chaucer's description of himself. Can it possibly be that the Wife of Bath is a portrait of Mrs. Chaucer?[30]

---

[28] See Robinson, pp. 727–28—note on CT, VI, ll. 72ff. If the reader is inclined to regard Chaucer's concern for the moral welfare of children as merely conventional, or what might be expected from any decent person, he may be referred to the astonishing data which Philip Ariès collected in his *Centuries of Childhood: A Social History of Family Life* (Knopf, 1962), Part I, Chapter V, on the deliberate cultivation of sexuality in children on the Continent at a much later date than Chaucer's.

[29] There is a useful summary of Chaucer's disclaimers in Marshall W. Stearns, "A Note on Chaucer's Attitude toward Love," *Speculum*, Vol. XVII (1942), 570–74. Mr. Stearns rejects Margaret Galway's view that Chaucer professed a chivalric devotion to Joan of Kent, widow of the Black Prince (see her "Chaucer's Sovereign Lady," *MLR*, Vol. XXXIII [1938], 145–99, and "Chaucer's Hopeless Love," *MLN*, Vol. LX [1945], 431–39), and takes the eight-year sickness spoken of in "The Book of the Duchess" as a conventional compliment to Blanche of Lancaster.

[30] *Chaucer* (Cambridge University Press, 1931); reprinted in his *Recent Prose* (Macmillan, 1933).

There are times when it is better to forego comment upon critical lucubrations.

The notion that Philippa Chaucer, like her sister Katherine Swynford, was a mistress of John of Gaunt (which would have been incest by fourteenth-century standards), and that, therefore, one or more of Chaucer's children were actually fathered by the duke, is not of recent origin, though it had fallen into what Grover Cleveland would probably have described as "inocuous deseutude" until Russell Krauss revived it in 1932.[31] Then, in 1965, George Williams published an amazing book called A New View of Chaucer, which I have already referred to in another connection, and which is certainly the most entertaining volume of its kind since Lillian Winstanley's eccentric interpretations of Shakespearean tragedy in terms of contemporary history. Mr. Williams' idea is that Chaucer married Philippa as a service to Gaunt, who had got her with child, this making the marriage purely a business arrangement. Williams considers himself a follower of Manly: "I have hardly done more than widen the road Manly laid out." He is referring of course to Manly's suggested identifications of the originals of a number of the Canterbury pilgrims in Some New Light on Chaucer. He also accepts the Manly and Rickert view that Chaucer studied at the Inner Temple and for good measure revives the tradition that he studied at Oxford also, with John of Gaunt paying the bills. But a good many readers, I fear, will entertain quite reasonable doubts as to the welcome Manly would extend to his new disciple.

Mr. Williams finds John of Gaunt and his affairs in practically everything Chaucer ever wrote. Never dogmatic, he does not insist upon his interpretations, but simply suggests that his hypotheses explain matters which have hitherto been obscure. His arguments are often extremely ingenious, and it is astonishing how many circumstances can be made to fit, though I think one may still balk at the notion that Chaucer himself was the original of both Pandarus and "hende Nicholas" in "The Miller's Tale."

---

[31] In Carleton Brown, ed., Three Chaucer Studies (OUP). Cf. Manly's replies, RES, Vol. X (1934), 257–73; Vol. XI (1935), 209–13.

Troilus, of course, is John of Gaunt, and Katherine Swynford is Criseyde. This would be more convincing if we had any reason to suppose that Katherine ever betrayed Gaunt, but, as Williams himself admits, we have none. Katherine and Gaunt were lovers for many years, and later, when it became possible, he married her and made her his duchess; if these two were not faithful lovers, and if their union was not "permanent," one hardly knows where to look for fidelity in the fourteenth century. Mr. Williams, however, thinks Chaucer may have thought Katherine was in danger of being deserted at the time of Gaunt's Spanish expedition; not only in the *Troilus* but in "Anelida and Arcite," "The House of Fame," *The Legend of Good Women*, "The Squire's Tale," "The Wife of Bath's Tale," and "The Clerk's Tale," Chaucer "seems to be waging a one-man campaign in the English court against any man who would forget his honorable obligation to his mistress." "The Complaint of Mars," too, is a plea for Katherine. Here, Mars is Gaunt, of course, and Cilenios (Mercury) is Chaucer himself, while the house in which Venus takes refuge is Chaucer's own residence at Aldgate. As I say, these are all fascinating hypotheses, ingeniously argued, but at present they can hardly be regarded as more than that, and the same thing must be said of the alleged skeleton in the Geoffrey-Philippa family closet.

One other sinister question mark has been set opposite Chaucer's name in connection with the strange case of Cecilia Chaumpaigne, who, on May 1, 1380, legally released him from any sort of action that might be taken against him *"tam de raptu tam de alia re vel causa."* Two months later, she also released Richard Goodchild and John Grove, who, in turn, released Chaucer of all obligations to them, and Grove promised to pay Cecilia £10 at Michaelmas.

In fourteenth-century English, *"raptu"* could mean either "rape" or "abduction."[32] (Chaucer's own father had been abducted by an aunt in an attempt to effect a marriage which would

[32] That the second meaning could have applied in 1380 has been denied in two articles in *Law Quarterly Review:* P. R. Watts, "The Strange Case of Geoffrey Chaucer and Cecilia Chaumpaigne," Vol. LXIII (1947), 491–515, and T. F. T. Plunkett, "Chaucer's Escapade," Vol. LXIV (1948), 33–36 (see below), but

have been financially profitable to her.) The Chaumpaigne mystery has caused much mental anguish to Chaucer scholars, but Paull F. Baum seems to be the only one who believes Chaucer to have been a rapist.[33] The three-sided nature of the transaction makes the degrees of responsibility that may have been involved particularly difficult to determine. Manly in his edition of *The Canterbury Tales* accepted the abduction hypothesis without even thinking it necessary to mention rape, and George H. Cowling saw Cecilia as "the victim of some Babes-in-the-Wood affair, in which Chaucer figured as the hero, with the armourer and the cutler [Goodchild and Grove] as the two villains of the piece."[34] The order in which the releases were entered does suggest that Chaucer was not the person most deeply involved. Those who witnessed his release were very distinguished men, and there is no evidence that he lost caste or fell into disrepute for whatever may have happened in 1380.[35]

A. C. Baugh calls their arguments "inconclusive"; see his *Chaucer's Major Poetry* (Appleton-Century, 1963), xv.

[33] *Chaucer: A Critical Appreciation.* What Baum states as conjecture in his "Note on Cecilia Chaumpaigne," pp. 41–43, becomes established fact on p. 133, thus illustrating a type of reasoning which is far too common among modern literary scholars ("for Chaucer himself had been up for rape, like the young Knight of the [Wife of Bath's] Tale, and they both escaped the death penalty . . ."). Freely admitting all the impenetrable obscurities of the case, Baum still declares that "there is no reason except Christian charity to whitewash the poet" (p. 42). Possibly "Christian charity" has larger claims than he seems to suggest, but the question of "whitewashing" is hardly involved, and the use of such a highly pejorative term in this connection is highly suspect. What *is* important is to form a reasonably consistent conception of the poet's character.

[34] *Chaucer* (Dutton, 1927), 23.

[35] Mr. Watts (see note 32 above) does not actually pronounce Chaucer guilty, but he does interpret the evidence so as strongly to indicate guilt, and his hypothetical reconstruction of Chaucer's relations with Cecilia and also with Goodchild and Grove certainly favors the hypothesis of guilt. He wonders, for example, "why Chaucer was not prosecuted at the suit of the King for the *raptus* of Cecilia Chaumpaigne. She must have made the incident the subject of open complaint; otherwise it could have been hushed up without the notoriety of a release under seal witnessed by the King's Chamberlain and other well-known persons and enrolled in Chancery." On Watt's hypothesis, I should think this a reasonable question. He cites as "one answer" Chaucer's "great influence at Court," which is, of course, itself hypothetical, from which he goes on to speculate on the possibility of Cecilia having been a consenting party and to certain speculations on the vagaries of the medieval legal mind which need not be summarized here. But he

Baugh remarks wisely of the Cecilia Chaumpaigne affair that "until more evidence is found the question remains open, and in the meantime it is best to suspend judgment." For my own part, I would add only that anyone who can believe the man who wrote the poems we know could possibly have been guilty of committing rape under any circumstances must be capable of accommodating far more complicated and contradictory notions of human character than I can.[36]

I have but one topic left to consider in this chapter, and this is what used to be called (before twentieth-century license in these matters not only caught up with but far outran Chaucer's)[37] the "problem" of the fabliau tales.

admits that the law being what it was, "a perfectly innocent man might prefer to settle the matter even at heavy cost to himself, rather than run the terrible risk of an adverse verdict." And he quotes J. W. Hales in the *Dictionary of National Biography:* "Whatever this 'release' may mean, it is certain that it brought no discredit on Chaucer in his day." Mr. Plunkett commits himself to another hypothesis—that Goodchild and Grove entered the case as sureties for Chaucer, to assist him in raising the money which Cecilia demanded. He concludes: "Finally, we must be fair to Chaucer. Rape is a brutal crime and implies a degree of depravity which should make us cautious in fixing such a charge. There is really no evidence for it. That he seduced Cecilia we may well believe; that she was angry with him, and thought that because it all happened against her better judgment, that therefore it was without her consent. . . . But there is nothing to suggest that Cecilia could have convicted Chaucer of felony. The single word in the close roll is the only word anywhere suggesting crime of any sort in this affair, and we must bear in mind that no one incurred legal responsibility for its truth. Doubtless there was some angry recrimination at the moment and hard words were used. It was unlucky for Chaucer's memory that one of them was engrossed in chancery." None of this is eminently unreasonable as hypothesis, and it would make an excellent foundation for an historical novel about the case. But it must be remembered that Chaucer did not live in an historical novel.

36 The only item in Chaucer that could possibly be cited on the other side of the argument is "The Wife of Bath's Tale," whose rapist-hero is punished much less than he deserves. But this is a story, and we all accept in fiction much that we would not accept in life. Gerould says this element was not used in any of Chaucer's analogues but does not attempt to make its use significant of anything about Chaucer, believing rather that it was intended to show that the narrator, the Wife herself, was sex-obsessed.

37 In 1962 "The Miller's Tale" appeared for the first time in a survey-anthology, intended for sophomore classes, and at least one teacher of my acquaintance introduced his students to Chaucer by assigning this story first. Yet in 1928 it was rather daring for Manly to include non-bawdy passages from the fabliau tales in his edition of *The Canterbury Tales* because he thought students should have some understanding of the realistic side of Chaucer's genius.

In the Middle Ages [writes W. W. Lawrence] physiological processes were taken very frankly. Sex had few reticences: it was not paraded, but was accepted with no blushes as a part of normal human life. The same was true of the excretory functions. Sexual and scatalogical decorations, some of them irresistibly funny, were common in churches and cathedrals and in the decoration of pious volumes. Sermons, didactic manuals, and books of edification contained stories which were, according to modern standards, rankly indecorous. There was little domestic privacy, even in the houses of the wealthy or the dwellings of the nobility.[38]

Lawrence does well to remind us that when, at the end of *The Canterbury Tales,* Chaucer retracts "thilke that sowned into synne," he is not thinking only, or perhaps even particularly, of the fabliau stories but of all that are not distinctively religious.

There is at least one "four-letter word" in "The Parson's Tale," and some of the fabliau stories end with benedictions:

> This tale is doon, and God save al the rowte!

and

> God blesse us, and his mooder Seinte Marie!

Robinson tells us also[39] that the Summoner's conception of the place which friars occupy in hell has been portrayed in ecclesiastical art.

The freedom of speech which medieval people practiced (and the strong stomachs which they possessed) are illustrated in "The Summoner's Tale" when the Friar, almost beside himself with rage at the filthy trick which the old churl has played on him, goes straight to the castle and tells his story *to the lord and lady as they sit at meat.*

> The lady of the hous ay stille sat
> Til she had herd what the frere sayde.
> "Ey, Goddes mooder," quod she, 'Blisful mayde!

38 *Chaucer and* The Canterbury Tales, 73–74.
39 P. 706—note on "The Summoner's Prologue."

Is ther oght elles? telle me feithfully."
   "Madame," quod he, "how thynketh ye herby?"
   "How that me thynketh?" quod she, "so God me speede,
I seye, a cherl hath doon a cherles dede.
What shold I seye? God lat hym nevere thee!
His sike heed is ful of vanytee;
I holde hym in a manere frenesye."

A Victorian lady would not have asked whether there was anything more, for she would have thought that she had heard far too much already. But Chaucer's lady of the castle is not necessarily less moral than the Victorian lady on that account, and it might well be argued that she is far more aristocratic. She knows the world, and it is no news to her that there are men in it who behave considerably worse than swine. It does not surprise her, consequently, when they do, but neither does it interest her, and she sees no reason why she should dwell upon or discuss the details.

Nevertheless there are problems connected with the fabliau tales, and Chaucer himself makes it impossible for us to ignore this. For he himself apologizes for them not once but several times.

The first apology is in the General Prologue:

> But first I pray yow, of youre curteisye,
> That ye n'arette it nat my vileynye,
> Thogh that I pleynly speke in this mateere,
> To telle yow hir wordes and hir cheere,
> Ne thogh I speke hir wordes proprely.
> For this ye knowen al so wel as I,
> Whoso shal telle a tale after a man,
> He moot reherce as ny as evere he kan
> Everich a word, if it be in his charge,
> Al speke he never so rudeliche and large,
> Or ellis he moot telle his tale untrewe,
> Or feyne thyng, or fynde wordes newe,
> He may nat spare, althogh he were his brother;
> He moot as wel seye o word as another.
> Crist spak hymself ful brode in hooly writ.

And wel ye woot no vileynye is it.
Eek Plato seith, whoso that kan hym rede,
The wordes moote be cosyn to the dede.

This is a fairly elaborate piece of self-justification, scurrying off in every direction to round up every conceivable argument of whatever nature that can possibly be made to apply. But the emphasis upon "vileynye" (discourtesy) would seem to indicate that the author thought his offense was less against morals than against decorum or "good form." And it may be significant that he follows this apology with another, much briefer one for not having "set folk in hir degree."

Before the Miller tells the first fabliau, Chaucer apologizes again, and this time he speaks of "harlotrie," admits the absence of "moralitee," and begs to be acquitted of "yvel entente":

What sholde I moore seyn, but this Millere
He nolde his wordes for no man forbere,
But tolde his cherles tale in his manere.
M'athynketh that I shal reherce it heere.
And therfore every gentil wight I preye,
For Goddes love, demeth nat that I seye
Of yvel entente, but for I moot reherce
Hir tales alle, be they bettre or werse,
Or elles falsen som of my mateere,
And therfore, whoso list it nat yheere,
Turne over the leef and chese another tale;
For he shal fynde ynowe, grete and smale,
Of storial thyng that toucheth gentilesse,
And eek moralitee and hoolynesse.
Blameth nat me if that ye chese amys.
The Millere is a cherl, ye knowe wel this;
So was the Reve eek and other mo,
And harlotrie they tolden bothe two.
Avyseth yow, and put me out of blame;
And eek men shal nat maken ernest of game.

This begins earnestly enough, but it ends almost frivolously (as if he got tired of arguing), with the suggestion that the matter is not very important after all.

Turne over the leef and chese another tale

is almost flippant (he seems to have been pretty sure nobody would), and

Blameth nat me if that ye chese amys

is like a sign on the highway advising the motorist that he proceeds at his own risk.

After the Miller has finished his tale, we have another passage which has received less attention than those I have already quoted:

Whan folk hadde laughen at this nyce cas
Of Absolon and hende Nicholas,
Diverse folk diversely they seyde,
But for the moore part they loughe and pleyde.
Ne at this tale I saugh no man hym greve,
But it were oonly Osewold the Reve.
By cause he was of carpenteris craft,
A litel ire is in his herte ylaft;
He gan to grucche, and blamed it a lite.

This seems to me a considerably more skillful and more impenitent justification than the others. Consider who some of these "folk" were—the Knight, the Prioress, the Clerk, the Parson, the Plowman. Since

Diverse folke diversely they seyde,

we may not assume that all were pleased without reservation.

But for the moore part they loughe and pleyde.

In other words, they agreed with the poet himself:

And eek men shal nat maken ernest of game.

Are you, Dear Reader, superior to the Knight, the Prioress, the

Clerk, the Parson, and the Plowman? If not, who do you think you are to object to what they listened to with equanimity? If you do, you may find yourself making common cause with the Reeve, who is just getting ready to tell a story equally bad, whose own morals will not bear examination, and whose reasons for objecting to "The Miller's Tale" are anything but disinterested. Evidently the gentles felt that when they made a pilgrimage in "mixed" (in every sense of the word) company, they must reasonably expect that not all their companions would adhere to their personal standards. So they listen to the churls' tales without censure though they would not have told such stories themselves. But when the Pardoner is called upon and prepares to cap the climax, they make it plain that enough is enough:

> "Nay, lat hym telle us of no ribaudye!
> Telle us som moral thyng, that we may leere
> Some wit, and thanne wol we gladly heere."

Hence the Pardoner is forced to think up "some honest thyng"— or to draw it out of his professional repertoire—while he drinks.

Kemp Malone argues that Chaucer's stated reasons for telling these tales are not to be taken seriously. As a counterirritant to some of the preternatural solemnity with which we have been regaled lately concerning the fabliaux, this seems to me excellent. Thus William A. Madden declares: "It seems to me likely that Chaucer intended the 'cherles' tales not only for their dramatic interest but also for the underlying seriousness of their implied comment on contemporary conduct." And Bernard Huppé reads "The Miller's Tale" as a commentary on "The Knight's Tale," which reveals "the confusion inherent in the view of reality which the Miller opposes to that of the Knight."[40] I wonder, though, whether Malone gives sufficient force to Chaucer's expressed concern for the integrity of characterization. If a writer of fiction is

---

[40] Madden, "Chaucer's Retraction and Mediaeval Canons of Seemliness," *Mediaeval Studies*, Vol. XVII (1955), 173–84; Huppé, *A Reading of* The Canterbury Tales.

going to create living characters, he must create the illusion of living speech, and the language which he employs must fit the teller. Otherwise,

He moot as wel seye o word as another,

for no characterization will emerge. This may be so commonplace to us that we pass it over without notice, but I wonder whether any other had perceived and enunciated it so early as Chaucer. Santayana would have scorned neither Chaucer's argument nor the particular application made of it. "Things called indecent or obscene," wrote the philosopher, "are inextricably woven into the texture of human existence; there can be no completely honest comedy without them." If Chaucer believed this, it would explain much which it is otherwise difficult to understand. Suppose he did enjoy "dirty" stories. Suppose he enjoyed them as much as some of his modern admirers do. Does this alone explain why he should have included them, in defiance of what his own words show that he regarded as certain forthcoming criticism, in his literary master-piece? Would he not, if that was all there was to it, have been more likely to content himself with telling such stories orally, at strictly "stag" affairs, as so many nineteenth-century gentlemen did? How-ever hypocritical these nineteenth-century gentlemen may seem to us, I am sure many of them would have been perfectly sincere in the horror and indignation they would have expressed had any-body tried to tell such a story before a lady. And one fancies that a good many of them never encountered the response which greeted one of the fraternity when, upon beginning with "I believe there are no ladies present," he was silenced by General Grant's "No, but there are gentlemen."

The problem of the fabliau stories in *The Canterbury Tales* is complicated by the point which Chaucer himself makes in the Introduction to "The Man of Law's Tale" regarding his refusal to tell stories about incest and kindred themes. The attempts which have been made to explain this as a hit at Gower, though hypo-thetical, are not unreasonable. If Chaucer was hitting at Gower here, he was hitting below the belt, for Gower had not written of Canacee and Appollonius of Tyre for salacious purposes (salacity did not lie within his range), and Chaucer was far too intelligent not to know this. By the same token, Gower, who had little humor and whose literary tastes were aristocratic, might have been expected to object to Chaucer's use of the fabliaux and may well have expressed his objection. And, to continue the chain of speculation, Chaucer might, thereupon, either seriously or playfully, have hit back by the suggestion that Gower had himself done something much worse than Chaucer could ever have considered doing. As I say, this would not have been fair, but men are not always fair when they are angry—or when they are mischievous either. Yet I cannot really believe that this elaborate hypothesis is necessary to explain the passage in question. Paul Ruggiers has noted that Chaucer "knows what it is to be human, sensual, and greedy as well as intelligent, and in all honesty he depicts the whole scale of behavior, *leaving out only the most depraved.*" It is a significant qualification, which could not be applied to modern fictionists, and perhaps Chaucer disregarded it himself when he created the Pardoner, though he certainly holds the balance even in his treatment of him. But different people—and different ages—have their own ways of being (if that is the word to use) prudish. "The Miller's Tale" is one thing, and the story of Appollonius of Tyre is another. Many an old-fashioned teller of barroom tales would have allowed his tongue to be pulled out rather than bring himself to discuss the perversions that are now spoken of openly in college classrooms and in mixed company.

When decency still prevailed in literature, the defense of Chaucer's fabliaux generally followed the lines laid down by Lounsbury:

> There is about the most objectionable of his stories nothing of that steamy licentious atmosphere which undoubtedy enervates the moral sense, even if it does not directly stimulate the passions. This is due in a measure to his outspokenness. Chaucer insinuates nothing, suggests nothing; what he means

he says without almost startling distinctness. Far more, however, is it due to the fact that the interest of the story as a
story does not depend upon the sin that enters into it.[41]

Though I have taken exception to the current tendency to read
"The Miller's Tale" as if it were a pious parable, I would certainly
admit that it should be obvious to every intelligent reader that the
tale is a product of Chaucer's mind and that Chaucer's mind was
not corrupt. The fabliau tales are not all of a piece. "The Miller's
Tale" is (as we sometimes say), "good clean dirt," redeemed, if at
all, only in the "riche gnof's" bumbling affection for his unfaithful
young wife—

> This carpenter answered, "Allas, my wyf!
> And shal she drenche? allas, myn Alisoun!"

and, even more, in the concern he shows for Nicholas himself,
when, as part of his plot to possess the Carpenter's wife, that
worthy pretends to be ill:

> "I am adrad, by Seint Thomas,
> It stondeth nat aright with Nicholas.
> God shilde that he deyde sodeynly!"

"The Summoner's Tale" achieves a refined and elaborated filth,
but there is a certain rough justice in "The Reeve's Tale":

> Thus is the proude millere wel ybete,
> And hath ylost the gryndynge of the whete,
> And payed for the soper everideel
> Of Aleyn and of John, that bette hym weel.
> His wyf is swyved, and his doghter als.

And "The Merchant's Tale," though the most disillusioned of all,
achieves a certain moral astringency through its very bitterness.
David Holbrook is quite right when he comments on the "gro-

[41] Bertrand H. Bronson, "Chaucer's Art in Relation to His Audience," notes the
following passages as exceptions to what he considers Chaucer's general freedom
from smirking: CT, I, ll. 2284–90 ("The Knight's Tale"); II, ll. 708–14 ("The
Man of Law's Tale"); IV, ll. 1950–51 ("The Merchant's Tale"); LGW, F,
ll. 148–52.

tesque and hideous" scene in the bridal chamber that "it is a marvellous comment on the terrible fact in human life of meaningless sex—and much human sex, when so depersonalized and loveless, must be thus meaningless." He adds: "When love comes to May it can only be adulterous love: but it is an awakening to life: the natural heart begins to grow as it could not under the merciless hands of January." Perhaps, after all, Proserpina was less cynical when she assisted her than has often been said.

V

RELIGION

In the fourteenth century it was almost as inevitable that an author who chose to write "of sondry folk" should send them off on a pilgrimage to Canterbury as it was that Oliver Wendell Holmes in nineteenth-century Boston should put them in a boardinghouse. Incidentally the difference between the two institutions points up the difference between two cultures. The fact that a man like the Miller, for example (not that there is a Miller in *The Autocrat of the Breakfast Table!*), makes a pilgrimage certainly does not show that he is, in any sense in which we would use the word, a Christian; the point is simply that while in our world he would not be having anything to do with the church, in Chaucer's time even such as he lived against a Christian background and in some sense breathed its atmosphere.

There may, however, have been a deeper reason why the pilgrimage background appealed to Chaucer. In "The Knight's Tale" he makes old Egeus say,

"This world nys but a thurghfare ful of wo,
And we been pilgrymes, passynge to and fro,"

and as a Christian he may well have remembered this. Nor need this have meant that he had less zest for the things of this world. Light shines most brightly against a background of darkness, and this remains true even if you believe that behind that darkness there shines a yet brighter light.

But *was* Chaucer a Christian? From where I stand the question seems a good deal like beating the air. But it has been raised, and it must be considered.

It was raised most emphatically, long ago, by Lounsbury, whose *Studies in Chaucer* set forth a vigorous argument in favor of the hypothesis of a skeptical Chaucer. "The evidence, so far as it exists, indicates that Chaucer's mind passed through several phases, but that towards the end doubt and denial became its leading characteristics." I doubt that all of Lounsbury's arguments would appeal to anybody today. From Chaucer's assumed skepticism concerning astrology and the existence of King Arthur, for example, Lounsbury concluded that he must have been a skeptic in religion also, and it now seems hard to believe that an intelligent man can ever seriously have advanced such an argument. Can Lounsbury possibly have supposed that Catholics are more credulous by nature than other people, that because they accept the Catholic faith they must accept everything else along with it? Is faith or unbelief a choice between believing everything and believing nothing?

Lounsbury also found "sometimes an audaciousness in . . . [Chaucer's] reference to the Supreme Being which can hardly fail to strike a discordant note upon the feelings of a man of strongly devout temperament." But I can find little or no irreverent intent in the example he cites, and I do not believe he made sufficient allowance for the difference between the medieval and the modern sense of reverence. (It is just as well, perhaps, that he never read Emily Dickinson, for he would surely have dismissed her as an atheist.) Criseyde's skepticism is no argument either, for she had no chance to believe in Chaucer's God, and she is not presented as a model for emulation. Nor do I find Lounsbury at all convincing when he makes either the Host or the Wife of Bath a mouthpiece for Chaucer's own dislike of clerical celibacy, though I must add that he could have disliked it without becoming therefore an unfaithful son of the church.

Moderns considering the question here under consideration would be likely to give more weight to the number of unworthy ecclesiastics that Chaucer created. At the close of "The House of Fame" he speaks of pilgrims, shipmen, pardoners, courtiers, and messengers, all with their boxes crammed full of lies, and of the male ecclesiastics who make the pilgrimage to Canterbury only the poor Parson and the Clerk (if he was already in orders) are entirely respectworthy. In addition, the monk in "The Shipman's Tale" is the lecher and a cheat, and the friar in "The Summoner's Tale" is both a glutton and a hypocrite.

Concerning the ecclesiastics there is still, perhaps, some difference of opinion. Fantastic interpretations of the character of the Prioress have been advanced in the past;[1] at present I do not believe any sensible reader would go further toward condemning her than Lowes did when he spoke of "the imperfect submergence of the woman in the nun." Most Chaucer critics seem to be of the opinion that Chaucer liked the Monk but disliked the Friar, a conspicuous dissenter being Howard Patch, who thought he liked them both. To me, on the other hand, nothing seems clearer than that Chaucer liked the Prioress but disliked both the men. I am willing to grant that the Friar was worse than the Monk; friars in general seem to have been in worse odor than monks in medieval England, and attempts have even been made to draw Chaucer into the controversies concerning them.[2] But surely the fact that Hitler was worse than Mussolini need not cause us to admire the latter. I do not see how any intelligent reader can doubt that both in the General Prologue and in what precedes and follows his own tale, the Monk is presented as a faithless religious, and it is quite beyond my understanding how anybody could read Chaucer's biting comments on his indifference to study without understanding that they are crammed full of heavy irony.

[1] These are reviewed, and quite effectively demolished, by Florence H. Ridley, *The Prioress and the Critics* (University of California Press, 1965).

[2] See Arnold Williams, "Chaucer and the Friars," *Speculum*, Vol. XXVIII (1933), 499–513, and Charles Dahlberg, "Chaucer's Cock and Fox," *JEGP*, Vol. LIII (1954), 277–90.

And I seyde his opinion was good.
What sholde he studie and make hymselven wood,
Upon a book in cloystre alwey to poure—

is this to be taken at face value from the man who wrote,

On bokes for to rede I me delyte

and

To rede forth hit gan me so delite,
That al that day me thoughte but a lyte?

While as for,

How shal the world be served?
Lat Austyn have his swynk to hym reserved!

how is the Monk serving the world—or God either—and what
kind of a fool do some of Chaucer's interpreters suppose him to
be? Surely John Speirs is right when he points out that " 'as he had
been anoint' contains within itself a contrast between the holy oil
and . . . [the Monk's] greasy fatness," and that " 'in good point,'
as might be said of a horse or dog, implies his animality."

Manly did not believe that the Monk was a sustained characterization, finding in the teller of the tale "distinctly a sedate and
bookish person, althogether different from the conception given
in the Prologue. Has Chaucer forgotten? Or did he change his
mind? Which conception is the later?"[3]

I doubt this interpretation. The Monk is not a "good" man, but
he holds a position in the community, he takes himself seriously,
and he does not permit gross familiarities to innkeepers and their
like. When he calls upon the Monk to tell his tale, the Host takes
unseemly liberties with him. He begins by commenting upon his
superb physical fitness, from which he passes on to open-eyed ad-
miration for his presumed sexual prowess. It is a great pity, he says,
that the Monk must live celibate:

"Haddestow as greet a leeve, as thou hast myght,

[3] *Chaucer's* Canterbury Tales, 635–36.

122

> To parfourne al thy lust in engendrure,
> Thou hadest bigeten ful many a creature."

The Host talks exactly like a modern believer in what we would
call eugenics. The trouble with religion, he says, is that it takes all
the strong men out of society, leaving only the "shrympes" to
reproduce themselves, thus steadily weakening the race. And the
moral effects of all this are equally unfortunate, for women naturally desire strong men, and since all the strong men are in orders,
they cannot have them legitimately.

Surely the Host is virtually accusing the Monk of having broken
his vows, but the latter is in no position to show resentment, for
he cannot put the shoe on without also admitting that it fits.

> This worthy Monk took al in pacience,
> And seyde, "I wol doon al my diligence,
> As fer as sowneth into honestee,
> To telle yow a tale, or two, or three."

He does not study now, but once upon a time he did, and he still
has "an hundred" tragedies in his call; so he mounts the high horse
of his dignity and trots them out, or as many of them as the company can bear to listen to. But at last the Knight interrupts him,
and Harry Bailly, who had expected a very different kind of story,
more in keeping with his true understanding of the Monk's character, seconds the objection in his usual brash style.

> "Youre tale anoyeth all this compaignye.
> Swich talkyng is nat worth a boterflye,"

and so on, down to

> "Sir, sey somewhat of huntyng, I yow preye."

But there is a limit to what the Monk will take from an innkeeper
and to his capacity to play "dumb." Then, too, he is probably less
sensitive about his hunting, which must be carried on openly, than
his more serious violations of the rules of his order.

> "Nay," quod this Monk, "I have no lust to pleye.
> Now lat another telle, as I have toold."

And the Host, unabashed, turns, with customary "rude speche and boold," to another, worthier cleric, the Nun's Priest.[4]

Why should Chaucer create so many unworthy ecclesiastics if he were a faithful son of the church? I should say because his England was, as everybody knows, abundantly stocked with just such ecclesiastics, and if Chaucer was ever what we should call a realist, he was one at the time he wrote *The Canterbury Tales*. Moreover, though Chaucer was not a religious reformer, he was both a humorist and a satirist, he knew the difference between right and wrong, and, like any writer of fiction, he reveals his own sense of values in the judgments he makes, explicity or implicitly, upon the characters he has created. His criticisms are all directed against abuses in the church, not against the faith, nor even against the organization as such. Not many characters in the General Prologue are idealized, but the Parson and the Clerk are; so are two other unclerical but intensely religious persons, the Knight and the Plowman. Certainly, whatever Chaucer may have doubted or believed, many medieval writers of unquestioned orthodoxy have criticized the corruptions in the church far more severely than he did. And they were better Christians and better Catholics for having done it.

Two of the passages which have often been cited as evidence of Chaucer's unbelief have now been quite effectively disposed of by Professor Roger S. Loomis.[5] The first is in "The Knight's Tale." When Arcite is killed, Chaucer writes (or the Knight says):

His spirit chaunged hous and wente ther,
As I cam nevere, I kan nat tellen wher.

---

[4] My views on this matter are, I should say, substantially in agreement with those which have been expressed by both Bertrand H. Bronson and Rosemary Woolf, but they were formulated long before I had read either of these writers. If it be objected to what I have written here that the conduct of the Prioress too was irregular, I can only reply that if it was (Sister M. Madeleva denies a number of the irregularities), the offenses involved are much less serious. The fun Chaucer pokes at the Prioress is very gentle fun. As a Christian he knew that she was not a saint, but since he himself was not a Pharisee, he would not reprehend her.

[5] "Was Chaucer a Freethinker?" in MacEdward Leach, ed., *Studies in Medieval Literature in Honor of Professor Albert Croll Baugh* (University of Pennsylvania Press, 1961). See also W. C. Curry, "Arcite's Intellect," *JEGP*, Vol. XXIX (1930), 83–99, who presents Chaucer's refusal to discuss the fate of Arcite's

Therfore I stynte, I nam no divinistre;
Of soules fynde I nat in this registre,
Ne me ne list thilke opinions to telle
Of hem, though that they writen wher they dwelle.
Arcite is coold, ther Mars his soule gye!

To the modern reader this does sound a bit skeptical, and even flippant, especially with the next verse reading:

Now wol I speken forth of Emelye.

Stylistically, this passage is not uncharacteristic of Chaucer, and when the devices he employs here work, they contribute notably to the delightful impression of colloquial ease which gives his work so much of its charm. But they do not always work, and I believe it is the passages in which they fail which are largely responsible for the reputation for "naïveté" which Chaucer once enjoyed. Professor Loomis seems to me to have made it quite clear, however, that in this case Chaucer is not expressing his personal doubts about immortality but rather referring to a question which was much under discussion at the time—What becomes of the virtuous heathen after they die? "It seems pretty clear that Chaucer preferred not to impale himself on the horns of that dilemma. In confessing his ignorance as to the house where Arcite's spirit dwelt, Chaucer was merely refusing to commit himself as to the fate of so noble a pagan as Arcite." And since he was not a theologian and could not speak for the church, he was being orthodox rather than unorthodox in taking up this position.

The other passage stands at the very beginning of *The Legend of Good Women* (F text), and there is much less excuse for its ever having been misunderstood, for in this case understanding requires only common sense, not specialized historical knowledge.

A thousand tymes have I herd men telle
That ther ys joy in hevene and peyne in helle,

soul as "based on artistic and philosophical grounds," partly, perhaps, by way of reaction "against the smug seriousness and general futility of scholastic dialect." But I cannot follow him when he goes on to suggest that Chaucer may have regretted having come close to spoiling the *Troilus* by adding the Epilogue.

And I acorde wel that it ys so;
But, natheles, yet wol I wel also
That ther nis noon dwellyng in this contree,
That eyther hath in hevene or helle ybe,
Ne may of hit noon other weyes witen,
But as he hath herd seyd, or founde it writen;
For by assay ther may no man it preve.
But God forbede but men shulde leve
Wel more thing then men han seen with ye!
Men shul not wenen every thing a lye
But yf himself yt seeth, or elles dooth:
For, God wot, thing is never the lasse sooth,
Thogh every wight ne may it nat ysee.
Bernard the monk ne saugh nat all, pardee!
　　Than mote we to bokes that we fynde,
Thurgh whiche that olde thinges ben in mynde.
And to the doctrine of thise olde wyse,
Yeve credence, in every skylful wise,
That tellen of these olde appreved stories
Of holynesse, of regnes, of victories,
Of love, of hate, of other sondry thynges,
Of which I may not maken rehersynges.
And yf that olde bokes were aweye,
Yloren were of remembraunce the keye.
Wel ought us thanne honouren and beleve
These bokes, there we han noon other preve.

Chaucer is not discussing a religious problem in this passage; he is discussing a scholarly problem—a question of evidence. We know nothing about the past from our own experience, he says; we know only what we read in books. If books were no more, racial memory would perish with them.

> Wel ought us thanne honouren and beleve
> These bokes, there we han noon other preve.

He is arguing for faith, not against it, faith in historic records. And to clinch his point he takes an illustration from religion. We have been taught

That ther ys joy in hevene and peyne in helle,

but we have never been in either place; hence we cannot tell from our own knowledge. So far from questioning the religious belief, *he regards it as axiomatic*. He is using the fact that we do believe

That ther ys joye in hevene and peyne in helle

as an argument for also believing other things of which we have no personal knowledge. Faith is needed in religion, but we must remember that it is needed in other areas of human life also. There is no suggestion of religious skepticism anywhere in this passage.

But there is another passage which has frequently been cited to prove Chaucer's alleged skepticism, and about this I cannot be quite so dogmatic. It occurs in the portrait of the Summoner in the General Prologue. The Summoner is a rascal, who will never haul an offender into the bishop's court if he can make more for himself by letting him go.

> And if he foond owher a good felawe,
> He wolde techen him to have noon awe
> In swich caas of the ercedekenes curs,
> But if a mannes soule were in his purs;
> For in his purs he sholde ypunysshed be.
> "Purs is the erchedekenes helle," seyde he.
> But wel I woot he lyed right in dede;
> Of cursyng oght ech gilty man him drede;
> For curs wol slee right as assoilyng savith,
> And also war hym of a *Significavit*.

In other words, the Summoner is a heretic who denies the spiritual authority of the church. The bishop has no jurisdiction over your soul, he tells his cronies. All he can reach is your money. If you are condemned by the bishop's court, the worst thing that can happen to you is that you may have to pay a fine.

Since it is often possible to express dramatically or in jest an

unpopular opinion which a writer would not dare put forth seriously and *in propria persona*, it is quite true that if Chaucer entertained heretical ideas on this point, he might conceivably have
chosen to get them expressed in this way. And then, to protect
himself and cover his tracks, he might have entered a disclaimer in
his own person. It could even be that

> For curs wol slee right as assoilyng savith

was meant to be taken at face value by the knowing ones in precisely the opposite sense to that in which it would be understood
by simple souls and that Chaucer meant that both were equally
effective in the sense that both were worth nothing at all. On the
other hand, the statement of the Summoner's belief might have
been reported solely as an element in his characterization, and
Chaucer might have added the disclaimer because he meant it and
because he did not wish to be associated with the Summoner's
heresy. The choice is ours to make, and we must make it in the
light of unambiguous passages elsewhere and in accord with
whether we believe that Chaucer was a believer or an unbeliever.
I do not believe that a writer who wished to propagate an unpopular idea would help himself very much by associating the idea with
so villainous and repulsive a character as the Summoner, especially
when he permits him to make at least one statement which is obviously not true upon any basis. The authority of the bishop's
court was not limited to levying fines. It could also imprison.[6]

Chaucer's distinctively religious references are numerous. I do
not mean conventional references to Christian institutions; these
he could hardly have avoided. But he has other references which
are not conventional. He was not essentially a religious writer, yet
he turned out much distinctively religious matter. In *The Canterbury Tales* alone we have three saints' legends, plus the *exemplum*
which is "The Pardoner's Tale," and the pious treatises which

[6] Muriel Bowden (*A Commentary on the General Prologue to the* Canterbury
Tales, 269) makes the effective point that Chaucer could not possibly have been
humorous in what he says of the Summoner's control over the young people of
the diocese. The influence of such a man could only have militated toward corruption, and for Chaucer the corruption of innocence was not among the
pardonable sins.

comprise "The Tale of Melibee" and "The Parson's Tale." In these last two there is nothing of an aesthetic character to sugar-coat the pill, and Chaucer assigned the first to himself and the other to one of the pilgrims whom he greatly admired. Moreover, Chaucer not only translated Boethius but came close enough to getting it by heart so that he recalled its great passages whenever he thought deeply about religious and philosophical problems. So did he also recall Dante, as we have seen, and *De Contemptu Mundi* and the Bible and the great Offices of the church.[7] Of course he is familiar with the great cardinal doctrines of the Christian faith, which he expounds directly in "The Second Nun's Tale" and refers to elsewhere so as to imply perfect familiarity with them whenever he needs them, as when, lamenting that Constance has no "champioun" he adds a reference to him

> that starf for our redempcioun
> And boond Sathan (and yet lith ther he lay).[8]

Chaucer also has many informal and incidental remarks, not necessitated in any way by the situation in hand, which it does not seem that a man unaccustomed to thinking in religious terms would have been likely to make. Of the music of nature in "The Parliament of Fowls" he writes,

> Of instruments of strenges in acord
> Herde I so pleye a ravyshyng swetnesse,
> That God, that makere is of al and lord,
> Ne herde nevere beter, as I gesse.[9]

[7] See Robinson, 734—note on "The Prioress's Prologue." Gordon Hall Gerould, *Chaucerian Essays* (PUP, 1952), points out that the prayer which begins "The Second Nun's Tale," though patterned on "Paradiso," XXIII, was neither a translation nor a paraphrase. "Dante's verses were refashioned or, it might be better to say, new-fashioned, shot through with echoes from hymns with which he was so familiar that the source of a particular phrase might well have been almost as elusive to him as to us. . . . The fact that Chaucer used part of the very same passage from Dante as the basis for one stanza of the prayer put into the mouth of the Prioress . . . further emphasizes the depth of its impression upon him and the value he set upon it." The fullest study of Chaucer's use of Boethius is in Bernard L. Jefferson, *Chaucer and the* Consolation of Philosophy *of Boethius* (PUP, 1917).

[8] *CT*, II, ll. 634-35.   [9] Ll. 197-201.

In "The House of Fame," bewildered by his strange surroundings, he turns instinctively to Christ:

> "O Crist!" thoughte I, "that art in blysse,
> Fro fantome and illusion
> Me save!"[10]

Even Troilus, who is not a Christian, is sure of one thing, when bewildered by the mysteries of foreknowledge and free will, that it would be "fals and foul, and wikked corsednesse" to hold an unworthy view of God.[11] The Canon's Yeoman probably is a Christian in the conventional sense, though he is certainly not a good one, but even he insists, in concluding his tale, that God's blessing is necessary for any great success:

> For whoso maketh God his adversarie,
> As for to werken any thyng in contrarie
> Of his wil, certes, never shal he thryve,
> Thogh that he multiplye terme of his lyve.

It is worth noting, too, that the fifteenth century thought of Chaucer as a pious writer, and that this tradition antedated the misinformed sixteenth-century view that he had anticipated the Reformation, which was based upon the erroneous ascription to him of works with which he had nothing to do.[12] "I ne knew never god but oon," he wrote in "The Book of the Duchess," and whatever he may have meant by that, it is clear enough that the God he knew was the God of Jesus Christ. There is a "glow" about

[10] I, ll. 492–94.

[11] TC, IV, l. 994.

[12] See George R. Stewart, Jr., "The Moral Chaucer," *Essays in Criticism, University of California Publications in English,* Vol. I (1921), 9–109, which long antedated the now currently fashionable attempts to interpret Chaucer in strongly religious and ethical terms, and without falling into any of their vagaries. Bertrand H. Bronson (*In Search of Chaucer*) insists, rightly, I think, that Chaucer was less the realist than many contemporary critics would make him. " 'Her is non hoom, her nis but wildernesse,' he wrote in his ballade, 'Truth'; and, so believing, he was unable to put forward his deepest meaning in terms of the data for everyday existence. It is no accident that it is the fabliaux that are the most drenched of all his pieces in naturalistic detail. They are the most *earthly* of his writings, and, by the same token—apart from morality in the narrower sense—in his eyes the most limited and least valuable."

Chaucer which seems distinctively Christian, and which, though he was certainly no saint, may remind us that "radiance" is one of the criteria which the church sets up for sainthood. It appears notably in such passages as the beautiful prayer to the Blessed Virgin which precedes "The Prioress's Tale," which breathe a religious fervor one can hardly believe to have been simulated.[13]

Some minds will no doubt be found impervious to this line of reasoning, but those which are not will be more impressed by it than by anything which can be weighed in a more exact balance. One such was Howard Patch, who had much to say that is worth hearing on this subject,[14] and who was impressed that in the famous passage at the end of the *Troilus*, the first thought that came to Chaucer was that Christ died for love.[15]

This and the Retraction at the end of *The Canterbury Tales* deserve special consideration in connection with our theme. In the Retraction Chaucer repudiates everything but his specifically religious writings; in the *Troilus* the emancipated hero looks back upon the earth he has left, to say farewell to love, after which the

[13] The best commentary on Chaucer's prayers is Sister M. Madeleva's in the title essay of *A Lost Language*. "The first and the last thing that Chaucer wrote was prayer. It finds its proper place in works between." There may be some special pleading in what Sister Madeleva writes about the Prioress ("Chaucer's Nuns"), though even here, her intimate knowledge of the life of a religious gives value to her essay. The special dictinction of her work in general is that she is probably the only ranking Chaucer scholar who can read Chaucer's religious writings in quite the spirit in which the author writ. She points out that philosophy is the general subject of Chaucer's prose works. "More particularly they deal with ethics and metaphysics: the consolations of philosophy, the seven deadly sins, contrition, confession. This was due neither to lack nor inaccessibility of other material. There were libraries of lays and legends from which to choose; encyclopaedias of stranger things than ever could be dreamed of in his philosophy; physiologies yet more wonder-filled; metaphysical mirrors and primers in plenty of the seven arts. . . . Chaucer was clearly more practically interested in the doctrine and use of the sacrament of penance than in many other matters of the day."

[14] *On Rereading Chaucer*.

[15] My argument could be bolstered considerably by reference to such interpretations of "The Nun's Priest's Tale" as are summarized by Robinson, p. 751, but I cannot say that I really find the "pan-allegorists" convincing or think what they do necessary. On the contrary, they seem to me inclined to misrepresent Chaucer as seriously as the sixteenth-century Protestants did. See Donald L. Howard, "The Conclusion of the Marriage Group: Chaucer and the Human Condition," *MP*, Vol. LVII (1960), 223–32.

poet himself urges the "yonge, fresshe folkes" who read him to give their hearts

> To thilke God that after his ymage
> Yow made, and thynketh al nys but a faire
> This world, that passeth soone as floures faire.

> And loveth hym, the which that right for love
> Upon a crois, oure soules for to beye,
> First starf, and roos, and sit in hevene above;
> For he nyl falsen no wight, dar I seye,
> That wol his herte al holly on hym leye.
> And syn he best to love is, and most meke,
> What nedeth feynede loves for to seke?

Together with "Truth" and other later short poems, these passages have often been taken as indicating that Chaucer, at the end, was taken with so narrow a form of pietism that he wished to repudiate nearly everything for which modern readers value him and that he looked back upon a lifetime which has left us all forever in his debt as a lifetime invested in the service of vanity. And Thomas Gascoigne has recorded:

> Thus Chaucer before his death frequently cried out, "Woe is me, woe is me, because I can neither recall nor destroy those things which I sinfully wrote concerning the base and sinful love of men for women, and which now will be continually circulated among men."

This may all be so, but it would not be necessary to make any such assumption to explain such statements. As Tatlock and others have shown, there is an "apologetic tradition" which has embraced writers so different from each other as Bede, Jean de Meun, Boccaccio, Spenser, Sidney, Herrick, Dryden, Ruskin, Ibsen, and Toistoi.[16] Andreas himself wrote not only *De Amore* but also *De Reprobatione Amoris*, in which he "replaced the natural and rational conception of man of the *De amore* with the

---

[16] Tatlock, "Chaucer's Retractions," *PMLA*, Vol. XXVIII (1913), 521–29; see, further, Robinson's note, p. 772.

Christian conception of man as a supernatural creature, a child of God by grace, with an end wholly different from the natural beatitude he had proposed in the *De amore.*" One stands "exclusively on the level of reason and nature," the other "on that of faith and grace."[17] Even theologians have been drawn into the apologetic tradition, and we have St. Thomas Aquinas dismissing his *Summa* as "rubbish."

To say this is not to say that Chaucer's retractions were "merely conventional" or that he "did not mean what he said." Nor is it to say merely that Chaucer, like other human beings, was a creature of vast complexity, and that different and, in some aspects, inharmonious sides of him had to be satisfied in his life and in his work. A work of art is not created by syllogistic rules, and if Chaucer could have a Criseyde whose fate was determined by the stars but also by her own character, I can see no insuperable objection to her being innocent by courtly love standards and at the same time guilty by Christian standards. But though he may very well have been capable of holding opposed views side by side on some subjects, I doubt very much that he could ever have agreed with Keats that "the only means of strengthening one's intellect is to make up one's mind about nothing—to let the mind be a thoroughfare for all thoughts, not a select party."

What he was sure of, as a Christian, was that man is both a spiritual and a physical being—or, as Rufus Jones expressed it in a more homely way, an amphibian—and that while he is on earth, he must live on both planes together. In one way or another, the physical and the spiritual must develop some temporary working scheme of peaceful coexistence; otherwise, a human being must choose between living a purely sensual life on the one hand and becoming a hermit in the desert on the other. Virginia Woolf was a good Platonist when she spoke of a woman's beauty as "only something flying fast which for a second uses the eyes, lips or cheeks of . . . [the woman herself] to glow through." Chaucer

---

[17] Alex J. Denomy, "The Two Moralities of *Troilus and Criseyde,*" *Transactions of the Royal Society of Canada,* Vol. XLIV, Sec. 2 (1950), 35–46, reprinted in Shoeck and Taylor, *Chaucer Criticism,* II.

could never have been so uncomprehending as Mark Twain was when he expressed his wonder over the anomaly that man who enjoys sexual intercourse beyond anything else in this life should have fashioned for himself a heaven from which sex is excluded. He would have known that it is precisely because sex is so greatly enjoyed here that it, along with every other purely earthly good, must be excluded from the life toward which we aspire, and that otherwise there could be no need of anything beyond.

There is, therefore, no real contradiction between the body of the *Troilus and Criseyde* and its conclusion; there is only a shift in point of view. Woodrow Wilson once told a critic of his policies that he was bringing the "white light of the Gospel" to bear upon the case, and that in that light nothing that was merely human could stand. There is no reason why a Christian may not view human life and activities with a perfect, comprehending sympathy (Christ himself did so), but he must always be aware of the difference between human standards and divine standards. Numerous passages in *Troilus and Criseyde* show that Chaucer always kept both ideas before him. James Fenimore Cooper admired his Indians, and Herman Melville admired the "savages" of the South Seas before they had been corrupted by contact with white civilization, but Cooper also insisted that while the Indian's "gifts" pleased God in an Indian, He would not accept them in a white man, and Melville was quite sure that, corrupt though civilization was, no white man could escape from it by "going native." Chaucer may not have been entirely consistent in *Troilus and Criseyde*, but he did include numerous passages which show that he realized his hero and heroine were pagans, and on the other hand he includes a good deal which reflects his own distinctively Christian basis of judgment.[18] Their love seemed "good" to Troilus and Criseyde—and, for all he says to the contrary, to Chaucer—while they were in the flesh, but once Troilus had become a spiritual being, then other standards of evaluation must be applied. I must say again that the fact that this was, from

18 Cf., with Robinson's notes where applicable, *TC*, I, ll. 1092–98; II, ll. 113-19; ll. 519–25, l. 1503; III, ll. 99–105, ll. 1576–82; IV, l. 623, etc.

the Christian point of view, a "sinful" love, or a love outside of marriage, had very little to do with the case. If they had been married, the ultimate judgment must have been just the same. There is simply a juxtaposition of this-worldly and other-worldly standards. The *Canterbury* Retraction is less prepared for, but even here the contradiction is not basic. As Chesterton, who doubted the authenticity of the Retraction, remarked:

> Even if Chaucer wrote it, it would not mean what a modern poet would mean by being ashamed of his poems. It would not mean that they were something specially bad on their own plane; it would mean that they were nothing on his ultimate plane: the plane of death and eternity.

And Paul Ruggiers adds that "what the Retraction spells out . . . is a statement of the limits of artistic experience." What Chaucer is saying is that "Poetry is insufficient." So, too, the learned Milton repudiated learning in *Paradise Regained*. I may add that I believe Chaucer's being a humorist may have made it easier for him to make the shift required to achieve this, for, to quote Ruggiers again, "it is the ultimate act of the ironist to pass judgment upon his own world."[19]

[19] Besides the references already cited, see, on this point, E. Talbot Davidson, "The Ending of Chaucer's *Troilus*," in Arthur Brown and Peter Foote, eds., *Early English and Norse Studies Presented to Hugh Smith in Honor of His Sixtieth Birthday* (Methuen, 1963); T. P. Dunning, "God and Man in *Troilus and Criseyde*," in Norman Brown and C. L. Wrenn, eds., *English and Medieval Studies Presented to J. R. R. Tolkien on the Occasion of His Seventieth Birthday* (George Allen & Unwin, 1962); Marion N. Greene, "Christian Implications of Knighthood and Courtly Love in Chaucer's *Troilus*," *Delaware Notes*, Thirtieth Series (1957), 57–59; S. Nagarajan, "The Conclusion of Chaucer's *Troilus and Criseyde*," *Essays in Criticism*, Vol. XIII (1963), 1–8; Charles A. Owen, Jr., "The Significance of Chaucer's Revisions of *Troilus and Criseyde*," *MP*, Vol. LV (1957), 1–5; James Lyndon Shanley, "The *Troilus* and Christian Love," *ELH*, Vol. VI (1939), 271–81; Theodore A. Stroud, "Boethius' Influence on Chaucer's *Troilus*, *MP*, Vol. XLIX (1951), 1–9. Shanley and Stroud are reprinted in Shoeck and Taylor, *Chaucer Criticism*, II, Shanley also in Wagenknecht, *Chaucer: Modern Essays in Criticism*. On the Retraction, see also A. P. Campbell, "Chaucer's 'Retraction': Who Retracted What?" *Humanities Association* [of Canada] *Bulletin*, Vol. XVI, No. 1 (Spring, 1965), 75–87, and in *Revue de l'Université d'Ottawa*, Vol. XXXV (1965), 35–53; also James D. Gordan, "Chaucer's Retraction: A Review of Opinion," in the Baugh book listed in note 5 above.

Of course none of this means that Chaucer never experienced religious doubt or that he was never tempted by any ideas that we would call heretical, for example, those of John Wycliffe. In the fourteenth century as in the twentieth, there was plenty of of religious doubt, and the only Christians who failed to think were those who were incapable of it. No reader of "The Knight's Tale," "The Nun's Priest's Tale," and *Troilus and Criseyde* (to mention no more) can be unaware of Chaucer's interest in fortune or destiny[20] and his numerous attempts to reconcile free will with foreknowledge (does the fact that God *knows* something is going to happen *cause* it to happen, and if it does what happens to the freedom of the human will and to man's moral responsibility?). Bernard L. Jefferson was impressed by Chaucer's uniqueness in leaving the question of free will open ("Boethius, Bradwardine, St. Augustus, Jean de Meun, and Dante all took sides one way or another on the problem"), and R. S. Loomis makes the point that "though Chaucer chose the way of faith and supported it with his translation of the *Consolation of Philosophy*, he does not, so far as I can remember, attack those who were lost in perplexity or who were vocal in their complaints against an omnipotent Deity." Both attitudes were, I think, characteristic of him. I doubt that he ever had much interest in metaphysical questions for their own sake. It was a working faith which interested him, and it was only when tormenting doubts got in his way that he seriously regarded them. Otherwise he was willing to leave them "to dyvynys." Like the Nun's Priest, he could suffer himself to be drawn away from the matter in hand by theoretical consider-ations, but like him, too, he could bring himself up sharply:

> I wol nat han to do of swich mateere;
> My tale is of a cok, as ye may heere.

And it was probably easier for him to do this because, even when he could not understand, there was always Mother Church in the background, and the universe need not stand or fall on his

[20] The authoritative study here is Howard R. Patch, *The Goddess Fortuna in Mediaeval Literature* (HUP, 1927).

solutions. "I know . . ." wrote Marjorie Bowen, on the last page of her autobiography,[21] "that sometimes I lose all . . . hopes and comforts and am overwhelmed by a blank melancholy. But even then . . . I can remember that where I have failed, thousands have succeeded, that what has escaped me, thousands have found."

The words I have just quoted are a woman's words, and the words of a woman who was not a Catholic, and they seem to me to express a distinctly feminine point of view. But I think Chaucer could have echoed them, for he understood women as few male writers have done, and had no difficulty in looking at the world through their eyes. Of all his philosophical passages, the most characteristic is the one he puts into the mouth of Dorigen in "The Franklin's Tale," musing over the cruel black rocks off the seacoast:

> "I wot wel clerkes wol seyn as hem leste,
> By argumentz, that al is for the beste,
> Though I ne kan the causes nat yknowe.
> But thilke God that made wynd to blowe
> As kepe my lord! this my conclusion."[22]

The "clerkes" think they know, and perhaps they do. Let us hope so; it is certainly desirable that somebody should know. But since they are not women, they cannot know what a woman feels, and so their knowledge is more or less irrelevant after all. Meanwhile, since there is a life to be lived, let us grant their knowledge provisionally and pray God to protect those who are dear to us. There is not much more that a woman—or a clerk—can do.

As for Wycliffe, Chaucer could well have had personal contact with him, and he was certainly acquainted with the Lollard knights who supported him. But this has little or nothing to do with his loyalty to the church, for the heresy issue was not clearly drawn during Wycliffe's lifetime. Nor would the fact that John of Gaunt was Wycliffe's special protector tend to tar Chaucer

---

[21] *The Debate Continues* . . . (Heinemann, 1939).

[22] Dorigen's entire meditation (*CT*, F, ll. 847–94), though too long to quote, should be read.

with the heresy brush, for Gaunt refused to go along with the reformer's more extreme positions. The Host's

> "O Jankyn, be ye there?
> I smelle a Lollere in the wynd,"

when the Parson rebukes him for swearing after "The Man of Law's Tale" is worth nothing as establishing Lollard or Wycliffite sympathy on the part of either the Parson or Chaucer, and anyone who thinks it does should be forbidden to read Chaucer or any other humorist. The Host is angry because he has been rebuked, and he strikes out by suggesting that the good priest is a "Lollard" in quite the same way that one of similar mentality in twentieth-century America might call an opponent a "Communist." The way in which that murderous pirate the Shipman immediately thrusts himself forward as a champion of orthodoxy, proceeding to tell a tale of his own to prevent the Parson's "springen cokkel in our clene corn," would alone suffice to show this. Obviously the Parson was the kind of parish priest Wycliffe admired, but while such men are not common in any group, we have no reason to suppose that all the faithful priests in Chaucer's England were Lollards or Wycliffites. Moreover, the tale which the Parson tells is strictly orthodox, revealing Wycliffite sympathies at no point.[23]

[23] The most elaborate argument in favor of the thesis that Chaucer was a Lollard is H. Simon, "Chaucer a Wicliffite," in the Chaucer Society's *Essays on Chaucer: His Words and Works*, Pt. III (N.D.); see also J. S. P. Tatlock, "Chaucer and Wyclif," *MP*, Vol. XIV (1916), 257–68, and, on larger issues, E. P. Kuhl, "Chaucer and the Church," *MLN*, Vol. XL (1925), 331–38, and Ezra Maxfield, "Chaucer and Religious Reform," *PMLA*, Vol. XXXIX (1924), 64–74.

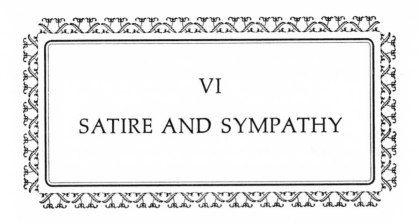

VI

SATIRE AND SYMPATHY

Satire and sympathy do not always go together, but in Chaucer both were developed to a high degree. His satire is all pervasive: he could see the funny side of everything Englishmen have generally agreed to hold most solemn. Puck's famous dictum would have suited him perfectly with only one word altered. He could have said with perfect propriety: "Lord, what fools *we* mortals be!"

Will Morpheus grant him sleep after his eight years' sickness? If he will, Chaucer will be ever so grateful. He will give great gifts to Morpheus—yes, he will give him a feather bed.[1] Friendship is a noble thing: Hercules would give his flesh and blood for Jason—if he might give them and still live.[2] Criseyde falls into grief, and her gossips stop in to comfort her. And they do comfort her—just as it would comfort a man who had a headache if you were to scratch his heel.[3] Moral indignation is inseparable from manhood, and no fate could be too black for the betrayer of women. Yes, indeed, and, as a matter of fact, no woman ought to trust any man—except, of course, Chaucer himself.[4]

[1] "BD," ll. 240–56. [2] *LGW*, ll. 1538–42.
[3] *TC*, IV, ll. 680ff. [4] *LGW*, ll. 2559–61 ("Phyllis").

He was a man of the court, and so when he becomes interested in reading Ovid he writes,

> This bok ne spak but of such thinges,
> Of quenes lives, and of kinges,
> And many other thinges smale.[5]

He was a learned man, perhaps a lawyer, and he shared the medieval fondness for the citation of authority. Therefore he must attribute a perfect passion for authority to the fowls in the barnyard, and in his portrait of the Manciple he celebrates that rascal's ability to hoodwink his learned masters, the lawyers.[6]

Taken by itself, all this would make for tartness. And a very sympathetic Chaucerian, Bertrand H. Bronson, has, indeed, recently, and, one gathers, somewhat to his own surprise, found that, in telling the story of the Canterbury pilgrims, Chaucer "depends on hostility for the dynamics of his 'drama.'" Certain pilgrims are associated with each other and said to be traveling in company, but "none of these is ever shown in friendly relations with another of his group, nor is any one of them ever heard to address a solitary syllable to his close companion." Furthermore, when the alignments among the pilgrims change in the course of the journey, it is always for the worse; the society in the *Decameron* "is not only more friendly but sweeter-natured." Yet Bronson himself adds that "such a spirit of geniality and good-humor pervades the *Tales* as a whole that the foregoing negative account will surely be resisted by most lovers of Chaucer, as belying the truth of his work."[7]

If this seems a curious circumstance, it is not a circumstance peculiar to Chaucer. Dickens is a genial and companionable writer, for example, yet how many of his characters are made contemptible through wickedness or foolishness! To be sure,

---

[5] "BD," ll. 57–59.

[6] Earle Birney, "The Beginnings of Chaucer's Irony," PMLA, Vol. LIV (1939), 637–55, points out many subtle examples of irony in Chaucer that are often overlooked. "So far, then, as our approximate knowledge of the Chaucer chronology allows us to judge, Chaucer was always an ironist."

[7] *In Search of Chaucer*, 61–65.

Dickens has plenty of good characters also, but are they not often less interesting than the rascals? I have actually had students who, in their examination papers, classified Mrs. Gamp with the "good" characters! Actually she has about as much benevolence in her as a rattlesnake, but she gives the reader so much pleasure that it is very difficult not to be grateful to her, and it is clear from his references to her in his letters that she awakened a certain wry, half-condescending affection in Dickens himself. There is a great deal in the Dickens world that is made tolerable only by the humor with which it is presented. His estimate of human nature was quite as clearheaded as that of a Swift or a Voltaire.

But Dickens was a reformer, and, like all reformers, he had his hard side. And Chaucer? If ever a man deserved to have that fine but much abused word "sweet" applied to him, surely it was he. George Herbert Palmer was impressed by the fact that though he had been taken prisoner by the French, he never expressed the slightest rancor towards France. "On the contrary, the imprisonment gave him an opportunity to know his sweet enemy, France, and to become better acquainted with French literature."[8] Manly speaks of his fondness for the word "merry," which he uses "almost with the freedom of slang."[9] D. S. Brewer finds a "calm, balanced, charitable personality" in his poems.[10] But nobody responded to Chaucer's centrality, balance, and wholesomeness more wholeheartedly than Lowell did or wrote about it more engagingly.

> Here was a healthy and hearty man, so genuine that he need not ask whether he were genuine or no, so sincere as quite to forget his own sincerity, so truly pious that he could be happy in the best world that God chose to make, so humane that he loved even the foibles of his kind.
>
> He could look to God without abjectness, and on man without contempt.
>
> If character may be divined from works, he was a good man,

---

[8] *Formative Types in English Poetry* (HM, 1918).
[9] *Chaucer's* Canterbury Tales, 640.
[10] *Chaucer and Chaucerians*, 246.

genial, sincere, hearty, temperate of mind, more wise, perhaps, for this world than the next, but thoroughly humane, and friendly with God and men.[11]

If it had not been for the satirical outlook which results from the humorist's perception of the wide gulf which yawns between human pretentions—or aspirations—and human achievements, this might well have led Chaucer into the bogs of sentimentality. If he escapes them, it is because he never pretends.

"It is not without significance," says William H. Scofield, "that he speaks of the 'gentleness' of 'the courteous Lord Jesus Christ,' and contrasts it with the 'vileinye' of the Devil." (For the notion that "the Prince of Darkness is a gentleman" lies outside the Christian tradition, and Chaucer did not subscribe to it.) Sometimes he represents himself as so overcome by his material that he cannot continue. After he reads the story of Seys and Alcione,

> by my trouthe,
> I ferde the worse al the morwe
> Aftir, to thenken on hir sorwe.[12]

He omits Dido's letter to her sister from her "legend"—

> So gret a routhe I have it for t'endite—

and having described the reunion of Constance and Alla, he declares:

> I pray yow all my labour to relesse;

---

[11] The quotations from Lowell are all from the famous essay on Chaucer in *My Study Windows.* One unpleasant question cannot be avoided: What of the Jews? Is "The Prioress's Tale," as we would say, anti-Semitic? I wish I could say no, but having made all allowance for Miss Ridley's demonstration that Chaucer omitted a number of points which a writer keen on blackening the Jews would have included, I still cannot find much charity in the tale. The best one can say for Chaucer in this connection is that he may well never have seen a Jew. If he had known Jews, he might well have liked them. But as the tale stands, they are Christ-killers, half-mythical monsters, set apart from the rest of humanity. And in "The Man of Law's Tale" he seems to take an equally dim view of Mohammedans.

[12] "BD," ll. 97–99.

> I may nat telle hir wo until to-morwe,
> I am so wery for to speke of sorwe.

Above all else, he was a man of good will. It is notable that practically every passage in which he shows any interest in politics includes a plea for mercy. In "Lak of Stedfastnesse" he does urge the quenching of extortion and stern exaltation of the law, but this is being cruel only to be kind. In "The Knight's Tale" he gives us the reasoning of Theseus, confronted with the problem of punishing Palamon and Arcite:

> And softe unto hymself he seyde, "Fy
> Upon a lord that wol have no mercy,
> But been a leon, bothe in word and dede."

Alceste, too, tells the God of Love that a king ought to be above petty resentment:

> Him oughte nat be tiraunt and crewel.

Gerould[13] and others have collected the lines in which he writes,

> For pitee renneth soone in gentil herte

and its variation,

> As gentil herte is fulfild of pitee.

It was his favorite idea. "Repeatedly, the plight of the innocent, of the deserted, of persons in one way or another caught inexorably by evil fortune or threatened with disaster is developed with tragic force. Only by sympathy and compassion is the dangerous life of man to be borne." He is kind in purely personal situations also, as toward the silly Carpenter in "The Miller's Tale" and the much less sympathetic Januarie in "The Merchants' Tale":

> He wolde so conforten in siknesse
> His squier, for it was a gentil dede.

In "The House of Fame" he wishes good dreams, success in love, and protection from want to those who read his poems but pro-

---

13 *Chaucerian Essays*, 83.

nounces a curse upon the malicious, the presumptuous, the hateful, the scornful, the envious, and the villainous.

In James Huneker's fine phrase, Chaucer was a "yes-sayer" to life. If he was less idealistic than some writers you might name, he had a heart upon which it would have been much safer to rely in a crisis than upon anything that many of the idealists possessed. He was not incapable of enthusiasm, but it was more characteristic of him that he should have been able to see even his most ardent partisanships in the light of that comic spirit which destroys so many things and which sweetens so many more. And Marchette Chute writes:

> Chaucer was almost incapable of picturing human beings as composing a class or group; he thought of them first as individuals. When Gower thought of the labor problem, Chaucer thought of a miller with a quick temper and a wart on his nose. When Gower thought of religious abuses, Chaucer thought of a pardoner with a love song running through his head and a glassful of "pigges bones" that he passed off as holy relics.[14]

This interest in the individual was what made Chaucer an artist —and a poet—for the poet is interested in life for what it is, and not for what he can make of it, as the scientist and the statesman are—but it was also what made him a humane man and a Christian. If he was not strenuous about changing the world, part of the reason was that it was God's world, and he loved it as it stood. He would have known what Jung meant by requiring of the psychotherapist "a deep respect for facts and events and for the person who suffers from them." This "unprejudiced objectivity" is "a moral achievement on the part of the doctor, who ought not to let himself be repelled by illness and corruption." But Chaucer did not need to learn this kind of thing from Jung, for he had learned it from St. Augustine.[15] And this, in turn, produced the

14 *Geoffrey Chaucer of England*, 200.
15 "Chaucer had it from St. Augustine that all created things are fundamentally

"large-minded serenity" which we all feel in him. "This serenity, in turn, seeks to describe rather than to prescribe, to accept rather than to reject, to understand rather than to judge, to forgive rather than to condemn."[16]

I should think that, generally speaking, he must have had a very happy life. There are indications, to be sure, that, like most of us, he had hours when he felt that the game was not worth the candle. Unfortunately, none of us can live steadily on the level of our highest perceptions or in the light of our highest faith. "The joyousness of his nature is unquestionably fully reflected in his productions," wrote Lounsbury; "but it is never the joyousness that springs from indifference or recklessness. Nor is it inconsistent with an undertone of melancholy. On the contrary, the refrain that recurs regularly in his writings is the transitoriness of happiness; that over the future of all of us the black shadow of calamity is ever impending."

> Criseyde loveth the sone of Tideüs;
> And Troilus moot wepe in cares colde.
> Swich is this world, whoso it kan byholde:
> In ech estat is litel hertes reste.
> God leve us for to take it for the beste![17]

The melancholy resignation is as overwhelming as it is gentle. And surely the saddest lines in English poetry are spoken by the dying Arcite in "The Knights Tale":

> "What is this world? what asketh men to have?
> Now with his love, now in his colde grave
> Allone, withouten any compaignye."

Only, this note never predominates in Chaucer. Like the Walter de la Mare who drew so distinguished a portrait of his Criseyde

good—that evil is parasitic, a deprivation of goodness rather than an entity; that one should on this account 'hate the vice but love the man.' " Donald R. Howard, "Chaucer the Man," 343.

[16] John Nist, "The Art of Chaucer: *Pathedy*," *Tennessee Studies in Literature*, Vol. XI (1966), 1–10.

[17] *TC*, V, ll. 1746–50.

in his early novel, *Henry Brocken*, Chaucer must have felt that we have no right to ask of the artist that he "shall answer each of our riddles in turn; 'tidy things up.' He shares our doubts and problems; exults in them, and at the same time proves that life in spite of all its duplicity and deceits and horrors, is full of strangeness, wonder, mystery, grace and power; is 'good.' "

And as long as spring came round each year, and so long as there were books to read, life must have been worth living for Chaucer. His tremendous curiosity alone would have kept staleness from ever coming near him. Almost all commentators have spoken of the gusto with which he describes, of all things, the sweating of the Canon's Yeoman:

> But it was joy for to seen hym swete!
> His forheed dropped as a stillatorie,
> Were full of plantayne and of paritorie.[18]

The indelicate lines have a spiritual value, for they furnish an index to a large and generous acceptance of life. And Aldous Huxley commented on how many, many things Chaucer finds it "joye for to seen," all the way from Criseyde and her maidens playing at ball to the Canon Yeoman's sweating. "The sights and sounds of daily life, all the lavish beauty of the earth fill him with a pleasure which he can only express by calling it a 'joy' or a 'heaven.' "[19] It was a pleasant way for a man to be constituted. And it is fortunate indeed that, having been born a genius, he should still be communicating his joy to us, more than six hundred years after what men call his death.

[18] *CT*, VIII, ll. 579–81.
[19] *On the Margin* (Chatto & Windus, 1926).

INDEX

The text for *The Personality of Chaucer* has been set on the Linotype in 11-point Electra, with two points of space between lines. Electra falls into the "modern" family of type styles, and with its inherent charm of design, provides new type-texture for book composition. It is the creation of the late W. A. Dwiggins. The paper on which this book is printed bears the watermark of the University of Oklahoma Press and has an effective life of at least three hundred years.